Central Texas Paranormal Society

CTPS
http://www.ctghost.org

Central Texas Paranormal Society

~Their History and Haunted Experiences~

Erin O Wallace

www.bookstandpublishing.com

Published by
Bookstand Publishing
Morgan Hill, CA
3357_3

Copyright 2011 by Erin O Wallace
All rights reserved. No part of this publication may be reproduced or transmitted in any form or by any means, electronic or mechanical, including photocopy, recording, or any information storage and retrieval system, without permission in writing from the copyright owner.

The author and CTPS members would like to thank Michael and Veronica Mangiapane for their contributions to the cover pictures. Plus a huge thank you to the talented Andrea Lopez (photographer) http://www.andrea-lopez.com and Dallas Lopez (graphic artist) http://www.dallaslopez.com for all their hard work in creating the cover of the book and bio pictures.

ISBN 978-1-58909-941-8

Printed in the United States of America

I wish to dedicate
This book in loving memory
Of my little lifesaver
And best friend,
Bernie Pearl Wallace.

Thank you my Jimmy!

The Central Texas Paranormal Society (CTPS)

Their Dedication

The CTPS would like to dedicate this book to all the people who are merely looking for answers. For all the insults, ridicule and rolling eyes we stand with you. Don't ever let it get you down. There are far more people who believe (but refuse to openly admit it) than those who do not. Stay strong and know that you are NOT alone in your quest.
We are here to help!

INTRODUCTION

After seeing a documentary about the Myrtles Plantation, which is considered to be "One of America's Most Haunted Homes", my youngest sister became extremely interested in the paranormal. Even though she's a confirmed believer in ghost and has always been intrigued by these unexplainable experiences, for some reason she began to want evidence. She and I had spoken about the supernatural and spirits many times. We both grew up around a psychic family member so it wasn't anything new to us. Knowing of my sister's new paranormal interest, I wasn't surprised when she suggested we visit such an eerie place. What I was puzzled about was her sudden desire to find proof of any ghost and spirits. She explained it was merely curiosity but I could sense it was something more.

I wasn't as interested in the paranormal as my sister. I was way more skeptical than her. However, the chance to visit a gorgeous plantation so rich in history did sound appealing. Since she felt this place might offer the answers she sought and I enjoyed historical homes, we decided to take a road trip. We packed our bags and headed to the Louisiana backwoods.

The moment we pulled into the gravel parking lot we knew there was something unique about this place. As we were checking in, we began to question the charming lady who worked behind the desk about the ghosts. Her name was Hester and she had the happiest eyes I've ever looked into. She smiled, winked and politely suggested we attend the historical tour of the Plantation coming up, as it would explain everything. Before we could even respond, we were greeted by the most captivating man. His name was Moses and I could sense a feeling of easiness when he looked at us. Hester introduced us to him and said that Moses was here if we needed any help during our visit. He walked us over to our room and told us to hurry because the tour would be starting soon. We raced to unpack and quickly got in line. Then, the plantation doors opened and we entered the most stunning reception area. The tour began and we were mesmerized. It was a beautiful home. When the tour was halfway through, I realized the tour guide was focusing mainly on the history of the house with no mention of ghosts. Towards the end, the guide finally spoke of several accidental deaths and murders that had occurred on the property years ago. We were allowed to see pictures of three apparitions that had been accidentally captured in a photograph by an insurance surveyor. The tour was interesting but mostly from a historical reference. We felt somewhat deprived of information on the haunting tales and a bit disappointed. Knowing what I know now, I'm glad she didn't reveal more during the tour. It left everything up to one's own discovery. This was a remarkably smart move on the tour guide's part for all of us. After the office closed, the house belonged to the guests. As nightfall approached, things started to change. There was an odd feeling in the air.

The grounds were dark, peaceful and quiet (except for the constant frogs croaking). It didn't take long before odd things began to come about.

We experienced numerous unexplainable occurrences. Our surroundings were engulfed with a strong, sweet floral aroma. It felt as though it was hovering over us. Then, as fast as it had arrived, it was gone. As an experiment, we asked if the spirits would make themselves known by quieting the frogs. Low and behold, they went silent in a blink of an eye. We took random pictures throughout the night and captured two orbs the size of children standing side by side. The most unsettling of all our encounters was the feeling that someone was hugging us whenever we sat in one of the porch rockers. Needless to say, there was little sleep going on that night.

As the weekend was coming to a close, we purchased a video of the plantation's haunting. To our amazement, the tales of the ghosts matched everything that had happened to us. Even the fragrance, the orbs and the hugs of the children were spoken of. Considering we were totally unaware of these accounts having been recorded, it made a huge impact on us. What began as a place to find answers, ended up resulting in more questions.

When we returned home, my sister was far more fascinated with the paranormal and I was no longer a skeptic. While the plantation left us with many questions, it did help guide us to a new phase in our lives. My sister discovered the Central Texas Paranormal Society (CTPS) group and from that point on we were hooked. Even though I am not a member of the CTPS investigation team, I do the historical research on the homes, businesses and the land which provides data to assist in uncovering the mysteries. I'm also the author of this book. I rely on the team to tell me what they stumble upon. As for my sister, she's still searching for her personal answers. At least now she has help. She signed on with the CTPS group and is now their case manager!

We both walked away from that pleasant yet frightful plantation completely changed people. However, together we are forever grateful. The experience opened doors and led us both on a new path we never imagined. Discovering the CTPS group has become the most fascinating turn of events for both of us. That simple visit to a "so called" haunted plantation has turned into a captivating journey. We now do historical research, uncover paranormal phenomena's throughout Central Texas, use the latest scientific investigation methods and work along side the most committed and professional team of investigators in their fields. I'm privileged to say, this is their story.

The CTPS Mission Statement

The mission of the CTPS is to help the public in understanding and dealing with paranormal activity occurring in their lives. This activity could be the result of something natural, but it may also be unnatural (spiritual) or for a lack of better word, paranormal (beyond the norm). Most people believe in a "Holy Spirit", but far less believe in worldly spirits. That being stated, the CTPS team is determined to find the truth and offer their explanation for the unusual behavior.

In all cases, the group strives to follow scientific methods to help establish the cause of the activity. Whether the source is natural or found to be paranormal, the CTPS will fully explain the results to the client. Copies of all documentation, images and/or recordings captured during the investigation will be provided to the client. If the cause is found to be paranormal, we will try to help the property owner understand the activity and deal with it in a way that is suitable in helping them.

First, teaching the client to live with the spirit(s) without fear and discomfort is our initial approach. If this is ineffective, then the next step would be to have the property blessed by our in house Clergy. This will help remove the unwanted spirit(s) and assist the spirit(s) in moving on. If this fails, the client will be referred to the Catholic Church for an official exorcism. Our team is composed of people of many faiths and we are all God fearing Americans. We believe in the "Holy Spirit" as well as the possibility of other spirits. The entire group are all devoutly dedicated in the pursuit for the truth to find out whether or not there is life after death.

Table of Contents

Author's Dedication		v
CTPS' Dedication		vii
Introduction		ix
CTPS Mission Statement		xiii
Table of Contents		xv
Chapter 1	How the CTPS Began	1
Chapter 2	Client Interviews and Research	5
Chapter 3	Performing the Investigation	7
Chapter 4	The Analysis	11
Chapter 5	Ridding a Ghost	13
Chapter 6	Meet the Team	17
Chapter 7	The Lorena Saddle Club	45
Chapter 8	The Mosheim Mansion	53

Chapter 9	Copperas Cove	63
Chapter 10	A Central Texas Hospital	69
Chapter 11	Lorena, Texas (Private Home)	73
Chapter 12	Penelope, Texas (Private Home)	77
Chapter 13	Author's Conclusion	83
Their Equipment		89
About The Author		93

Chapter 1

How the CTPS began

As with most skeptics turned believers, an unexplainable occurrence is usually the cause for having such a drastic transformation take place. No matter how skeptical one might be, after experiencing a paranormal encounter the layers of doubt quickly begin to diminish. The founder of the CTPS, Harry (known as "Pop" to the team) was no different than anyone else.

Pop considered himself to be "the poster boy for the nonbelievers". His usual response to someone speaking about ghost was "yeah right". Then in 1982, he and his wife, Karen (and two daughters) purchased a house with no known paranormal activities, at least none that they were aware of. Being a nonbeliever, inquiring about any possible ghosts in the house never crossed Pop's mind. Immediately after moving in, odd things started happening that they couldn't explain. It caused Pop some uneasiness, yet being such a skeptic he simply brushed the incidents aside. It wasn't until he was injured in an accident and laid up for several months that he was forced to take notice.

While home alone, he would hear talking, things were being moved around, doors opening and closing in other rooms, etc. Now Pop was growing more apprehensive. Knowing he would be returning to work soon and having to travel frequently, he began to worry about his families wellbeing. Even though the activities were merely annoying and not harmful, it was still a concern. For the first time, he began to wonder if maybe there really was something supernatural in his home. The bigger question was how does one go about discovering this? During the 80's, paranormal investigations hadn't been developed to the extent it is now and certainly not so willingly accepted. With no information to turn to, Pop and his family accepted the mysteriousness of their home and went about their day to day lives.

Since no harm was being done, the family grew accustomed to the bothersome activities. Around 1987 they were transferred to another city and sold the house. However, the curiosity for answers never left Pop's mind. Then in 2004, he retired after 24 years with the federal government. Suddenly, Pop was left with a lot of free time on his hands. Barely settled into his retirement, he came across a very interesting television show.

It was an episode of a ghost hunting type show. From that moment, something inside him sparked. Seeing there were now tools capable of capturing proof of ghosts, he knew this was something he wanted to pursue. Thankfully, everything had gone digital and equipment was readily available. Little did he know it wasn't going to be as easy as he thought.

Hearing of Pop's new interest, a friend of his mentioned her home was experiencing some paranormal activity. Eager to test his new ghost hunting tools he just purchased, he offered to check it out. Quickly the word spread and two of his three daughters, Becky Nagel and Lee Ann Smith, his grandson, Josh Smith plus two friends Pammie and Carolyn wanted to join in on this experiment.

Having no real knowledge of what they were doing, this first investigation was a complete bust. Their equipment consisted of two mini DV cameras, two digital still cameras and two voice recorders. The whole inventory of equipment fit in a laptop case with room to spare. Refusing to be discouraged, they began investigating cemeteries. This type of investigation was also unsuccessful.

Yet to no avail, Pop wasn't giving up. He had noticed that there were several paranormal groups on-line with web sites. He needed to get his name out and his new partner, Lee agreed. A web site seemed like a good start. Pop reached out to his long time friend, George who built web sites. To his amazement, George arranged to build one at a great price for him. Now he waited to see what this new exposure would reel in. He was astonished by the response. Pop had hoped to keep the team small using mostly family members and close friends. After seeing the numerous responses, he knew he was on to something big. His nephew, Robert and brother, Wiley wanted to join but lived to far away. Pop suggested they start a team under his banner and thus the Central and North Texas Paranormal Society were formed.

The CTPS was inundated with request from individuals to join and cases to be investigated. This meant a lot of interviewing. Through painstaking efforts, they were able to weed out the serious investigators from the people looking for a weekend form of entertainment. Pop and Lee considered themselves to be deeply dedicated researchers and weren't going to settle for anything less from their team. Several applicants were chosen and then trained. Now with a committed team by their side and cases waiting to be investigated, the new CTPS group got to work. Lee embarked on researching and writing case studies for the sites in questioned. She also added to their equipment out of her own pocket, as did Pop.

Hundreds of dollars for tools quickly turned into thousands. Pop soon learned that the right tools were not cheap or as readily available as first thought. Nevertheless, he believed his team could not do a good job if they didn't have the right tools. His philosophy is "Never ask a man to dig a ditch without giving him a good shovel." What tools his investigators needed, they got. There were no questions as long as they showed results. Plus, team members are responsible for the care and upkeep of any equipment used. No member ever disagreed.

After a couple of years of investigating, CTPS was still loading all their equipment in Pop's pickup and heading out to each site. Seeing the team growing and the cases were mounting, it was time to upgrade. Lee and Pop pitched in together and outfitted a trailer for use as their Mobile Command Center (MCC). This was an expensive but worthwhile investment.

They now set up their DVR systems, computers and even a coffee pot in the trailer, which they lovingly call "home sweet home". The CTPS group no longer worries about weather conditions or prying eyes. With the popularity of the numerous TV ghost shows, CTPS draws crowds where ever they go. Understanding the public's curiosity, a member will answer their questions then politely explain the team's need for privacy. For the CTPS clients' sake, they strive to maintain a controlled atmosphere. This is something they have become exceptionally skilled at.

When Pop was asked where does he see the CTPS heading in the future, he responded "Good question! I've always thought it was unethical to charge people for a service I provide. Since it is I who is looking for answers to an age old question, I feel as though I should be paying them. But in return for the privilege of looking for these answers in their homes or business' we help them solve or learn to accept their problem. I plan on doing this as long as my health will allow or we find those answers. I know I'll never become rich and famous or on a TV show since I have a face for radio. I'm not a writer or an actor nor am I willing to fake something this important. So with the help of a good team, I will just keep plugging away as long as someone out there thinks they have paranormal problems and need help or answers."

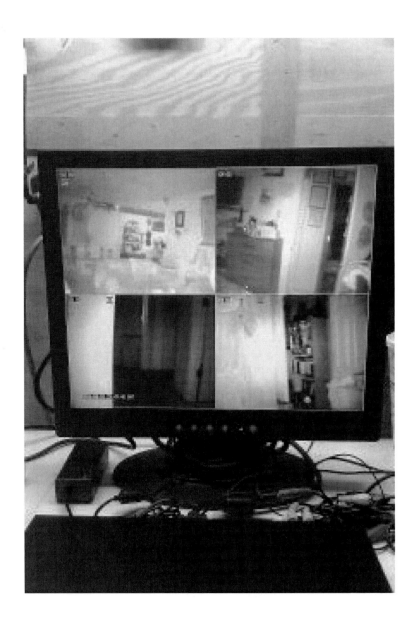

Chapter 2

Client Interviews and Research

CTPS receives numerous requests for investigations and each case is carefully reviewed for its merits. Just as the team protects their client's confidentiality, Pop and Lee look after their teams' safety. Each potential client is first given a phone interview, then a face to face discussion. You would be amazed how important a one on one interview is. As skilled paranormal investigators, they can decipher true fears from just the mind playing games. The lead investigator will thoroughly inquire as to what type of activity is causing the client's concerns, such as shadows, banging, cold spots and/or apparitions. If a genuine need is determined, then the research is set in motion.

The CTPS group has several team members who are knowledgeable in researching houses, buildings or land using various methods. Many times just by looking at a house or building can give them an idea of the structure's age. Going over the architectural drawing of a building is like looking at an old photograph. With a picture, the style of a woman's clothing, her hat, any cars in the picture, etc. is the same as the formal design of a building. These are all clues which can produce a time frame reference. After a quick inspection of the building in question, the hunt for a paper trail begins.

A search for a deed registration at the county clerk and recorder's office is the first stop. Reviewing the deed will offer the history of the purchase and its selling price. If a dramatic increase or decrease in the price or tax assessment is recorded over a short period of time, it usually means something has changed. This can range from either remodeling to fire or flood. Building permits are great for listing the type of structure, dates of construction and details. The prior owner's information can also be accessed.

If the previous owner is discovered, they will track them down by searching the internet. If the owner is found, the CTPS can get a better understanding of the original house. Of course, that depends on the age of the house and if the owners are still living.

The local libraries keep files of old photographs. This is a good spot for tracking down pictures of the house or neighborhood from past years. It gives a good reference of what's happened in the time since the pictures were taken.

The team then checks other public records based on owner's names, the address of the house, and any other information available.

Most often, an older house will pass from one owner to another through a mortgage or a will and won't show up on deeds.

If the house is historical and the haunt severe enough, surveyor maps in the assessor's office will be located to uncover if any rooms had been added or demolished. This office keeps records of the taxable value of the home, and there could be old appraisals on file that describe the house in great detail. A check of old city directories, county histories, vital statistics, and census records are another resource.

Once all resources are explored, the team researcher compiles the information to create a chronological description of the house. This shows how and when it was built, when various parts were added or demolished, and what natural events may have made changes to the house.

Understanding the history of a house, building or land is the same as getting to know a new friend. You can't fully understand their personality until you discover what they've been through. The saying "if only the walls could talk" is entirely accurate.

Chapter 3

Performing the Investigations

After interviewing the prospective clients and completing the research on the property, the next job is to set an investigation date. If the site is occupied by residents, they advise the clients they are not allowed to be present during the examination. The clients are asked to make other sleeping arrangements. If the property in question is a great distant from the team members' homes, they must also find other accommodations. Since all team members are volunteers, this expense is out of their own pocket.

When the scheduled date has arrived, the Mobile Command Center (MCC) is brought in and the painstaking task of setting up the equipment begins. CTPS has a large array of state of the art tools, such as Digital Hi 8 Cameras w/Infrared Lights, Infrared Remote Cameras, Wireless Videos, Laser Lights and Motion Detectors. Depending on the size of the property, arranging this vast inventory of gear can take up to several hours.

From the previous client interviews, the team is aware of the "hot spots" and where the activities have been occurring. The equipment is then positioned in those areas. With their two way radios, the team inside the MCC conducts a thorough testing of the equipment and confirms their proper placement. After placing hundreds of yards of extension cords and the coffee is brewed, they wait for Pop's approval. When given the thumbs up, the team bows their head for a beginning prayer. It is usually said as a group and sometimes to ones self. It is believed this is done for the protection of the team from unwanted spirits entering their bodies or following them home. It also sets the stage for a safe and peaceful evening for everyone.

Reverend Mark of the CTPS group has provided this prayer for the team **"Dear Lord,** our **Savior**, please protect those of us taking this perilous step into the unknown, and guide us with your wisdom, and all the blessings you may bestow upon us, and **Lord,** please keep us safe during the unforeseen outcome of this investigation. In **Jesus** name we pray, **AMEN".** The team finally embarks on their long awaited investigation. The investigators will be outfitted with such items as Digital Mini DV, Still Cameras, Thermal Imaging and Full Spectrum Cameras w/Infrared Lights, Digital Analog Voice Recorders, Electro Magnetic Field (EMF) Meters, Laser Thermometers, Infrared Night Scopes and Strobe Lights, Tri-Field and K2 Meters, Two Way Radios and mini Flashlights. Ghost or spirits are known to drain freshly charged batteries as an energy source, so plenty of batteries will be on hand. At this point, the fully equipped team will be sent in two at a time. These teams will be rotated throughout the evening giving all members an opportunity to experience any possible paranormal activity.

To produce the best results, silence is required during an investigation and is necessary in capturing an EVP (Electronic Voice Phenomena). Sounds can be registered very easily, so the team must be quiet outside as well. The weather plays an important factor during an investigation including movements of rustling trees, wind, thunder and other outside influences, as these will all be noted throughout the recording.

The teams of two will get comfortable using very little movement to make the spirits at ease. Each investigator has their own unique way of trying to communicate with the spirits. For the most part, the questions are all being aimed for the best results. When the investigators speak, their voices are in a louder tone than normal and clear to ensure the spirits hear them.

Each member begins their opening comments with their name, date and time. This gives the techs a sample of the team member's voice in case they need to exclude their voice during the EVP recording. The team will then invite the ghost to make them selves known. They suggest that banging on something or moving an item is helpful. Not every spirit is capable or desires to verbally or physically communicate. For those that do, some spirits speak loud and clear while others are barely audible. The team will explain to the spirits to speak as loud as possible to be heard and that every effort will be made to capture it.

When a team member asks a question, they give a 10 second pause before the next question. This allows the spirit time to slowly respond and to gain their trust. Not all spirits respond right away or at all. Remaining respectful is very important. The team always remembers, they are in the spirits home and upsetting a spirit only frightens them away. A comfortable setting provides more results. The team will ask such questions as; what is your name? How old are you? Where were you born? Do you live here? These types of questions tend to provide a more relaxed environment. As the evening wears on, the questions become more serious. Such as, how did you die? What year is it? Is something keeping you here? During the questioning, the area will be constantly monitored for any temperature changes and EMF fluctuations. The room will also be observed through the Thermal Imaging and Full Spectrum Cameras. If an investigator hears or see's something, they will make note of it for the techs who will be reviewing the tapes later. It can be a comment such as "Did you hear that?" "Was that a slamming door? " It's a point of reference for the tech who will be listening to the recordings afterwards.

During the entire duration of the investigation, the techs and lead investigator keep an eye on the team from the MCC using a DVR Surveillance System, four way monitors and computers.

When the evening begins to come to a close, the team thanks the spirits for their time before the team's departure. The spirits are also reminded to stay where they are and are not welcome to come home with the team. A parting prayer is then said: " **Dear Lord,** we thank you, for guiding us through this task, and keeping us safe, and secure in your arms as we traveled into the unknown, and **Lord** please guide us safely back to our loved ones at home, with only **your Spirit Lord** returning home with us. In Jesus name we pray. **Amen".** If a future visit is possible the team will actually tell the spirits they may be returning and invite them to join them. All the equipment is then gathered, packed up and the team heads home with an often successful story.

Chapter 4

The Analysis

After a lot of exhausting work and a well deserved night's sleep, everyone heads back to their own homes, families and routine day to day jobs. The results of these investigations are never uncovered overnight. It's nothing like you see on those television shows. It's a tedious, tiresome, difficult process that can last days or even weeks to accomplish.

All of the collected data from the investigation is downloaded to the CTPS computers which are equipped with a program called WavePad. This software was originally intended for music editing studios and professional journalists but has become a valuable tool for paranormal groups in deciphering EVP's.

When the evidence gathered has been entirely downloaded, the information is reviewed personally by Pop, Dana and Lee. Occasionally, other members will lend a helping hand when available. This process requires time, patience, sharp ears and keen eyes. Every micro inch of data is thoroughly scrutinized by this devoted team. Being the meticulous people that they are, they will always listen to the data more than once. Considering the multitude of the evidence they collect during an investigation, this is an incredible undertaking. If a suspected EVP is found, it is then confirmed by another member. The segment will be isolated, filtered (to remove background noise) and examined once again.

The EVP's are classified in several different ways. Class A EVP's are very clear spirit statements and there is no question of the message being sent. Class B EVP's are less clear but still easily identified after filtering any background noise. Class C EVP's are audible but very hard to understand.

The reviewers will pay close attention to any loud bangs or unusual sounds caught on tape. This is a common way for spirits to communicate. It's believed a spirit can be transported on the end of the wave created by the sound. When a banging sound is recorded, they will listen more intently to the end to see if anything has been captured. Pounding noises can also be words or actions that the spirits are trying to communicate. The team will then slow down or speed up the tapes in hopes of uncovering something. As soon as the audio portion of the evaluation is behind them, they will move on to the countless hours of videos and hundreds of still photographs.

The image recordings are given the same amount of attention as the audios and are just as daunting. All of the collected videos and photographs will be examined thoroughly for any shadows, mist, movement or anything unusual. If something is found, the segment in question will also be isolated and confirmed by another member. At the end of their task, anything captured from the investigation will be loaded onto a disc. A copy of this disc will then be given to the client and never shared by the CTPS group unless written permission has been granted. Even then, it is on a need to know basis.

Chapter 5

Ridding Unwanted Ghost

If the result of the CTPS's investigation reveals something possibly supernatural, the group will then make a decision on whether or not the ghosts are harmless or hostile. Their conclusions are based on the type of activity being produced by the ghost. The team will look for any unwelcome evidence such as, aggressive EVP's, heaviness in the atmosphere, or occupants being physically touched or hit. These are usually signs of something dark. Although this rarely occurs, it does happen from time to time. If this is the case, their in house clergy will be called in with hopes of banishing the offending spirit.

For the most part though, ghosts are not dangerous. A good number of haunts are residual energy in nature. This means that it's similar to a video or audio that plays in a loop with no ability to connect or stop. As for the ghosts that do have the capability to interact, they are simply curious or looking for attention. Learning to live with the ghost is the best route to take. All it requires is an open mind and patience. Coming to an understanding with a harmless spirit will help both parties be able to coexist. The few steps needed to achieve this are very simple.

Think about a ghost as merely a long term guest. Request the same guidelines of them as you would of any visitor in your home. The CTPS team recommends keeping in mind that the house does not belong to the ghost, it belongs to the current resident. Their best advice is to be assertive and make the ghost aware that they are not the one in charge. The owner must lay down the law in a forceful, strong manner to cause the ghost to take notice. Then announce to the ghost that if they wish to remain there, they must not be bothersome any further. It's important to let the spirit know they are welcome to stay, as long as they abide by the rules. Maintaining an attitude of "this is my home, not your's and that's the way it is" works wonders.

If the client is uncomfortable living with the ghost and would like for it to leave, there are a few ways to go about accomplishing this. Unfortunately, there are no guarantees. Not all ghosts are willing to simply disappear. The CTPS will first ask the client if they are certain they wish for the ghost to go away. What if it's a relative or friend of theirs that has passed on just wanting to spend time with them?

This is something they may not have considered. If they insist on removing the ghost, they will suggest to the client to state in a firm clear tone that it is time for him or her to move on and that this is their home now. If after several attempts this doesn't help, the CTPS will carry out an ancient American Indian tradition called smudging. This is a purification method where white sage is burned in a conk shell. A feather is waved over the shell spreading the smoke throughout the dwelling. During the entire ritual, prayers are continuously repeated. Every room will be treated, as well as the exterior of the property. On some occasions this will work but again there are no guarantees. If this process fails, the CTPS will advise involving the church. The team's resident clergy, Reverend Mark will be brought in to make his own attempt of ridding the ghost.

Some clients may wish to invest in the use of a psychic. Many psychics are skilled in the ability to help release a spirit and assist them in crossing over. This is a service not provided by CTPS and can be very costly. It is completely at the client's own discretion. The CTPS group is determined to help resolve any issues the ghost or spirits may be causing and are willing to invest as much time as necessary. Ridding a ghost can take days, weeks or even years. As long as the client is willing to hang in there and not give up, the CTPS team vows to do the same.

Chapter 6

Meet the Team

Lee - Co-Founder of CTPS/Lead Investigator/Case Manager - Her first encounter was at the age of five, when her grandmother (Nonnie) passed away. After the funeral, she fell asleep only to be awakened by a presence in the room. Although she didn't see anyone, she knew it was her grandmother. Without uttering a word, Nonnie somehow communicated that she was fine and not to worry. Then closing the door behind her, she was gone. Years later, Lee shared this touching story with her mother. As tears began to well up, her mother explained that Nonnie had visited her that night as well. Sadly, being so frightened by the visit, she had asked her to leave. Lee believes her Nonnie visited her to help guide her to the path she's currently on. Since then, she's had numerous encounters with paranormal phenomena's, yet not all so pleasant.

Such as the night while sleeping on the sofa, she woke up petrified with the feeling of being pinned down and unable to move. The room was cold and the air still. Once panic set in, the sensation was gone. From then on, the atmosphere of that house was uncomfortable. Items would disappear, then turn up later and unexplainable shadows would be seen. Then one day, Lee got the shock of her life. She came face to face with an apparition. It was a wild looking man with bushy, matted hair and crazy eyes. After such a frightful encounter she was determined to get to the bottom of this. Lee researched the history of the house and made a horrifying discovery. The previous tenant died in that house from a drug overdose. Fearing for her child's safety, they quickly moved. Now, living in a one hundred year old house she could not be more comfortable. Though coming across spirits in her new home, they are peaceful. Lee is at ease cohabitating with ghosts who mean no harm and believes it's possible to co-exist with spirits. She feels there's no need to be afraid if you just open your mind to see what's there.

Becky - Field Investigator. At a young age, Becky experienced something so profound it changed her life forever. During the middle of the night, she entered her mother's empty bedroom. As she looked towards the bed, she saw a woman sitting who she didn't recognize. As she walked towards the woman, she could sense somehow that she knew her. The woman calmly began to gesture for her to come closer. Once approaching her, she was given the most affectionate hug. She was compelled to lay her head on her lap. The gentle woman began to stroke her hair as she apologized for missing her birth. She explained how she had so wanted to be there. Then she spoke of Becky's future and reassured her that although it might be difficult at times, it wouldn't last forever. After a brief conversation, they said their goodbye's and gave each other another hug. As Becky was leaving the room, she turned around for one more glimpse. The kind woman was gone. Even at such a young age, she knew this was something supernatural. As Becky grew older, she had convinced herself this had been a guardian Angel. Then one day she was looking through some old photos when she came across one that took her breath away. It was a picture of the same woman she had encountered in her mother's bedroom. When she questioned her father about the woman in the photo, he explained she was her great grandmother who had died before she was born. Overwhelmed by her discovery, she shared the story of her childhood encounter with her father. All they could do was smile. Looking back now, this experience had given her a delightful memory and filled her with contentment. She has been forever grateful for her visit.

Now a USAF wife, mother of four and grandmother of one, she believes we all have a soul. God gives us the knowledge to return to earth to visit loved ones but sometime's we get lost along our way back to heaven. Her belief is that with a little understanding, anyone can overcome their fear of the unknown. Becky hopes that by her being a member of the CTPS team, she might be able to pass this along.

Dana- Field Investigator/Evidence Analysis. Dana's first encounter with the supernatural was at the age of four. Her family lived in an older two story home with an attic that could be easily accessed. Although the room was unfinished, it was a magnificent place for a child to play in. While her brother was at school, she would have it all to herself or so she thought.

One afternoon as Dana was playing in the corner of the attic, she was startled by something extremely bizarre. Suddenly, an opening like a large window appeared right in front of her. She can still remember vividly looking at this mysterious object. With no sense of danger, this tiny four year old girl put one foot on the bottom of the structure and held onto the sides. As she stepped through the porthole she reached out into a mist that seemed like spinning clouds. The light was bright and the sky was swirling. When she turned around, a beautiful, dark haired little girl wearing a wispy, pale blue dress stood in front of her. Although the girl didn't say anything, Dana knew her name was "Mazine". She recalls having a long conversation with her. From then on, they were best friends. They had countless tea parties, played with dolls, and cut out paper dolls. The attic became Dana's special play house. Her parents knew that children often had invisible playmates, so they weren't concerned. They had no idea their daughter could actually see her.

When Dana was six, her family moved away from her beloved home. Only to have Mazine move with them. By this time, her parents were growing tired of the "invisible playmate routine". Dana knew she had to ask Mazine to leave. She remembered telling her playmate that her parents were getting upset with her visits and that she had to go. It saddened Dana to have to do this, but it had to be done. Mazine would return several times tempting Dana to talk to her. Sadly, she would say "No Mazine, you have to go". Then one day she finally stopped appearing. Even though Mazine no longer shows herself to Dana, she can still feel her presence. As an adult, Dana has often thought about her special companion. She wonders "who or what was she and did she have a purpose? Was she a ghost or her guardian angel?" She was certainly her friend, but how does this all fit into her belief system, especially her religious beliefs. Dana states "What I have found is that although most people don't like to admit that unexplainable things have occurred in their lives, (because they are afraid someone might think they are unstable). Once you reveal that something extraordinary has happened to you, almost everyone has a story of their own."

Shelley – Case Manager/Field Investigator. One of Shelley's closest family members studied the subjects ESP and Ghost Phenomena. For her, paranormal activities and conversations about the supernatural were an everyday way of life. Growing up around such an environment was difficult for a child but helped lesson her fear of the unknown as she matured. When asked what her first experience with the supernatural was, she recalled seeing the "handsome tall man" (whom she lovingly named). He came to visit her when she was around six years old while she was playing in her room. The man resembled her father who was still living, so there was a sense of trust present. When she walked towards him to speak, he simply vanished. This brief encounter would not be an isolated event. The man would become a regular visitor throughout her life as if watching over her. Now a grown woman, she continues to see and even hear the tall man from time to time. In her eyes he has become her guardian angel and dear friend.

This type of supernatural dealing would not be her only occurrence. One other such encounter was the time her family member was testing out the use of anagrams with a group of ESP researchers. As they began their study, the group deciphered the letters to read "a little red headed girl wants to be your friend". From then on, a red headed little girl was seen at the end of Shelley's bed numerous times. A few years later, Shelley and her family were about to be transferred to another area. Surprisingly, the night before they were scheduled to move away, the little girl came to say goodbye. She was never seen again.

As Shelley grew older, her curiosity about ghost and spirits was strengthened. Could someone actually come back to visit if they so desired? Is it possible to visit our own children and let them know we're here? Can we really continue to watch over our love ones? These are the answers Shelley seeks. Being at ease with spirits through her experiences so early in life, she wants to help educate others that there is so reason to be afraid. Her knowledge, calming way and eagerness to learn more in the field of paranormal research and analysis strengthens the CTPS group. Shelley states "I feel very close to spirits because I can sense they are close to me as well. It also helps to have a good team by my side. The CTPS group makes me feel very safe at our investigations. I've learned so much from them and look forward to every investigation".

Tracey- Lead Investigator/Co-Founder Northwest Texas Paranormal Investigators (NWTPI). Tracey is by far the most unique member of our group. First, she is one of three sisters. But not just sisters, they're triplets. That certainly puts her in an exclusive group of people right from the start. On top of that, Tracey has a very special paranormal awareness. She can best be described as the young character from the movie called "Sixth Sense". She sees dead people. Although her encounters were never as frightening as the young boy's, the over all depiction is basically the same.

The supernatural world has become a normal way of life for Tracey. When asked what her first paranormal experience was, she replied "to be honest, I can't remember not having one. It's all I know. Even though I never asked them to appear, they've always sought me out." She recalled seeing full body apparitions and shadow people walking through the halls of her elementary school during her classes. Black masses would form and linger on the walls. These type of episodes were so natural to her they never caused her any concern.

Tracey remembered how the evenings would be the most active time for her ghostly visits. She'd hear voices calling her name as she tried to sleep. Her bed would shake as if someone was trying to wake her. There would be the feeling of tugging on her arms and legs, disturbing her sleep. Even strange bright lights would appear in the dark of night. Tracey tolerated a constant sense of a presence, even in an empty room. The only paranormal capability that would test her emotional strength would be the ability of knowing when a loved one was going to pass away. Recognizing this was something she couldn't alter, the stress of these premonitions would be draining.

As Tracey grew older, she wanted to share her paranormal experiences and knowledge accumulated over the years with those who needed it most. While living in Amarillo, along with Michael and Tim, Tracey founded the Northwest Texas Paranormal Investigators (NWTXPI). Their main goal was to help ease people's fear of the paranormal world. She wanted to spread the word that by understanding what you fear, it's less hard to be afraid of. After three years of working along side the NWTXPI team, she had to transfer to Killeen to be closer to one of her sisters. With spending so much time collecting evidence and learning about paranormal investigation, it didn't take long before she grew to miss it. Once she settled into her new surroundings, her search for a new paranormal group promptly began.

Sifting through the numerous paranormal societies' information, she landed on a web site that caught her attention. The logo read "We are here to help!" It was the web site of the CTPS. Reading over their mission statement and previous investigations, their philosophy resembled hers. Needing more information before she decided, she contacted the group. Pop would be the first member she'd speak to. Through their conversation, she was impressed by his intense questioning of her. Pop was direct, meticulous and genuine. This gave her a feeling that this was a leader who took his job serious and a strong protector of his team. Tracey immediately signed on for an investigation.

Several months later and dozens of investigations behind her, Tracey asked Pop why he was so hard on her during their first conversation. He stated "The CTPS isn't just a paranormal investigation team. We're a family. I'd never let a stranger into my home unless I was certain they meant us no harm. Trust has to be earned. It's not something I easily give away." Then he turned to her and said "welcome to family, Tracey." Needless to say, she has been a member ever since.

Tracey's duties involve documenting paranormal activity to verify its existence. Through deductive reasoning, she attempts to clarify why such activity may be occurring. By doing so, she hopes that scientific proof may someday be discovered and that the existence of ghosts or spirits will be found. She strives to help the public and those who live with paranormal activity deal with certain fears and misunderstandings they may have.

Robert (Robbie) - Lead Investigator/Director of D/FW Paranormal Sister Team. He is the CTPS team's rock star, as they like to call him. Robbie is a member of numerous groups. In addition to being a member of the CTPS, he is the Director of his own paranormal group based in northern Texas. This multitalented person is also a musician with his own band. He is also a machinist specializing in stainless steel polishing, a husband and a father of two children. The team is lucky to be able to have Robbie find time to assist them with their investigations.

Robbie's interest in paranormal investigation was awakened by the popular television show called "Ghost Hunter International". Purely by a twist of fate, he landed on a marathon showing of various episodes one Sunday morning. Having never seen the show before, he was captivated by it. Robbie was so fascinated by the evidence they found and the possibility that ghost might actually exist he watched every episode throughout the day. Before then, he never gave the reality of ghost or spirits a second thought. He had a few incidences when he was young, but never really connected the dots as to whether it was paranormal or not. After viewing these thought provoking episodes, it brought up a lot of uncertainty for him. As with most, when a paranormal event has been experienced the wheels of curiosity begin to turn. Even if it's in the form of a television show, once the consideration that there may be life after death is sparked the questions pile up.

From that point on, Robbie wanted proof for him to see if this show's discoveries were truly factual or merely embellished. The only way to find out was to research this for himself. Like all amateur paranormal investigators, the first thought was "where to begin". Surprisingly, he discovered his uncle, Pop had recently started his own paranormal research group. Amazed by this coincidence, Robbie asked to attend an investigation.

Being a family member, Pop agreed to let him tag along on one of their jobs without hesitation. Thinking this was just a passing interest, Pop treated him as he would all visiting guest by putting him straight to work. Robbie was required to follow the same mandatory guidelines that all the skilled CTPS investigators have to follow. Pop believes if you're going to be a part of the team, then it's necessary to pitch in. For the strapping young man this was no problem, he dove right in. As with most investigations, dead time starts off slow and this one wasn't any different. Once the early hours of the morning came, the unusual activity started to begin.

The investigators began to experience an abundant amount of unexplainable happenings. Seeing this as a perfect opportunity for Robbie to

take in what the seasoned investigators go through, the team led him into the most active area. It didn't take long and he got his first encounter. While standing far away from anyone else, Robbie was hit in the side of his body with an unexplained force. He was stunned. At that exact moment, another member's digital recorder was slapped right out of their hands. For most novice investigators, this would leave them running for the hills but not Robbie. This brawny guy turned to face the unknown and said "Bring it on, I'm not going any where". The CTPS team instantly knew Robbie was to be their newest member.

When Robbie was asked why he decided to join the CTPS group, he kindly answered "I love helping people in anyway I can. After working with the CTPS group, I discovered they'll do everything possible to help those troubled by something they can't see. They're honest, caring and hard working individuals who are sincerely concerned about people in need of help. I know this is where I belong. They've become my second family. The paranormal world is a mysterious thing to comprehend but trust me when I say, it's very real. Once you personally experience something paranormal, your whole outlook on life is different. The equipment CTPS uses is very scientific & sophisticated. It helps reveal things we can't hear or see with our own ears or eyes. Believe me, what I've seen & heard was unimaginable but real. I am now a true believer. I thank God, my family and my uncle for giving me this opportunity."

Wiley - Field Investigator. Unknown to Wiley, some CTPS team members refer to him as the "Quiet Man". The phrase comes from the title of an old movie about an ex-boxer who hangs up his gloves vowing never to fight again. No one really knew of the character's past and his calm persona helped hide his immense inner strength well. The character in the movie was a gentle, quiet and caring soul. But if pushed to hard, the gloves would easily come back on. This is Wiley's personality through and through. He is considered to be the team's gentle giant who is willing to protect every one of his friends, family and team members. Knowing Wiley's got their back, brings a sense of peace and security to their investigations.

Having been with the team for nearly three years, he is one of their more skilled investigators now. Wiley had no paranormal training before he joined CTPS. Being an Aircraft Machinist by trade, supernatural research was the furthest thing from his mind. His introduction to paranormal investigating came by way of his brother, Pop. Although Wiley never gave much thought of life after death even existing, he was intrigued by his brother's ghost hunting interests. After certain investigations, Pop would talk with Wiley to discuss his fascinating stories of eerie encounters and the unbelievable evidence captured. During one of their thought provoking conversations, Wiley suddenly remembered a frightening experience he had endured at the age of eleven. Having been so profound, he wondered how he could have ever forgotten it.

Wiley recalled it had been a cold winter's evening. He had fallen into a deep sleep, when suddenly he was awakened by a severe jolt. He felt a strong grip around his ankle and then an aggressive yank of his leg. The force nearly jerked him halfway off the bed. When he looked up to see who had done this, no one was there. The event was so violent all he could do was cover his head with the blanket and wait until daylight. Fearing his parents wouldn't believe him, the next morning he reluctantly told his family about the incident. He was amazed to learn he had not been the only family member to witness something bizarre. His grandmother had also been a victim of an unusual event.

That same night, Wiley's grandmother had just fallen asleep when she was awakened and startled by a loud noise. She quickly raised her head to look out her opened door which led into the kitchen. To her disbelief, she could see a ghostly flame standing on top of the stove. It was about four feet tall with a shape resembling a person floating in the air. Thinking there must be a gas leak or that someone had left the stove on, she rushed towards it.

As soon as she got close to it, it simply disappeared. She was horrified by this. The family being so frightened and confused by this mind boggling episode, they never discussed the subject ever again.

Until his conversations with Pop about paranormal investigations, Wiley had completely forgotten about this incident. Now after recalling it, he couldn't let it go. It's odd how a long ago paranormal ordeal can hide in one's mind, stirring up truth-seeking questions. Wiley was to be no different than anyone else who went through a supernatural incident. He wanted answers and joining the CTPS team was the best way to find them. Since then, he has been on nearly every investigation. He has even founded his own paranormal sister group based out of Arlington.

Wiley was asked if he's found the answers to his questions yet and he replied "I'm not sure I'll ever truly find what I seek. I can say that it's comforting to know there's another side to death and that we are definitely capable of communicating after the life we've known is over. Through my investigations with CTPS, I've gotten numerous EVP's, have been physically touched and have had things knocked right out of my hands. These personal experiences have made a true believer out of me. My belief now is that spirits do exist and they only wish to be acknowledged or assisted in passing over." Wiley went on to say how proud he was to be a member of CTPS. Not only does he love the thrill of the paranormal hunt, he very much respects his fellow investigators and enjoys working with them. He hopes to continue performing paranormal research for the rest of his life.

Reverend Mark - Field Investigator/Reverend. Mark and Pop have been best friends for over a decade. After a few investigations, Pop shared some of his experiences with Mark. The stories were so fascinating, he was overwhelmed with curiosity. This deep interest then turned into uncertainty about things he had never doubted before. His individual belief is straight forward and uncomplicated, there is a holy spirit and unfortunately an evil spirit. But for the first time he asked himself "Why just these two spirits?" This simple question has now become a full blown personal and spiritual challenge for Mark to comprehend.

As Pop and his team began to delve further into paranormal investigating, Mark also notices the challenges they were facing. As a spiritual leader, he recognized their need for religious support. He felt he could bring comfort to the team by reminding them that the Lord was with them, not only during the investigations, but in their day to day lives as well. Once Mark joined the team, there was a sense of safety and comfort. Mark would remind them before every investigation that the Lord is their savior and caretaker. He promised to listen to the teams words, as well as speak the Lord's word to them. As the group's spiritual leader, Mark confirmed the importance of finding the truth about the afterlife. He encourages the group to not be afraid.

Then one day, Mark's words would be tested on himself. While attending his first investigation at a home in Ferris, Pop and Mark entered one of the bedrooms in the home. Something just didn't feel right to them. As Mark slowly opened the door, he could feel an extreme chill in the air. Since it was in the middle of a Texas summer this was beyond belief. As they made their way out towards the hall to enter the front living room, Mark started to talk to Pop, halfway into his sentence he stopped. He could feel something trying to enter his body. Being a clergyman his natural instinct was to grab the cross he wears around his neck and say a prayer. As soon as he finished the prayer, the spirit left his body. Struggling to finish his sentence, Pop asked him if he was ok. As he was trying to explain what had just happened, Pop brought him to the MCC to rest. The analysis' crew began to review the recordings, in hope that something had been captured. During that conversation between Mark and Pop, a large orb traveled from the bedroom and went right into Mark's body. It remained for a few seconds, then left his body and exited right out the front door.

Now Mark is positive he needs to remain with the team. He feels this is where he sincerely belongs and promises to protect and listen to the

team's words, as well as speak the Lord's word to them. Mark states that "Ghost hunting, inquiring into the supernatural world, spirit chasing or what ever you may call it is very interesting. It's challenging, fun and is definitely one of the true unsolved mysteries of the world. I want to be a part of this incredible journey and am honored to be a member of the CTPS team".

Rita - Field Investigator/Video Specialist. Rita was actually too young to remember her first encounter. It would be her mother who would share this most unusual story with her. When she was scarcely a toddler, her parents were attending a funeral and brought her along. While at the cemetery, she accidentally wandered away from her parents. As her mother was desperately looking for her, Rita found a comfortable shady spot to sit. Then she was approached by someone she would refer to as the "no name person". They would end up having a long conversation together. After franticly searching for what seemed like an eternity, Rita's mother finally found her. She was sitting peacefully on top of a grave having a chat with someone only Rita could see. Although bewildered by her child's strange conversation with no one, she was extremely grateful to find her unharmed. To this day, her mother believes it had been a guardian angel protecting her little girl.

As Rita grew older, she began to have unusual dreams. During her sleep, she would dream of several deceased family members and friends. They would come for a visit to reminiscence about the past and speak of the future. The visitors would warn her of problems on the horizon and talk of pleasant things to come. Her late grandfather (who she had been very close to) would be the most frequent guest. Rita noted the deeper her sleep, the stranger the dream. They were beginning to feel more like visions instead of dreams. She couldn't understand what this all meant. It wasn't until her husband was called back to Desert Storm that she began to make a connection.

With her husband called back to war, Rita was consumed with fear. She had two young children and was frightened he might be killed. Having just suffered the loss of a dear friend as well, she felt vulnerable and alone. Shortly after her husband was deployed, her deceased friend came to visit through a dream. It was as though she was truly awake. The dream was so real and peaceful. Rita let her know she missed her and how afraid she was for her husband's life. She couldn't bear to be left alone with two children. Her friend spoke but a few words, "It's going to be okay in one week." The dream faded away then suddenly everything around her seemed different. To Rita's amazement, exactly one week later the announcement came that the war was over. Her husband was to be sent home. This experience convinced her she was having what was recognized as REM premonitions. Knowing she had someone watching over her, gave her a feeling of tranquility and a sense of security. After this incredible experience, Rita's revelations while sleeping would soon take a turn in a different direction.

Shortly afterwards, her visions would go beyond her dreams and become a reality. Her first encounter would be the time her step father had just passed away and she was at her mother's house. As her back was turned towards the bedroom door, she could feel someone watching her. When she turned around, she saw fingers slip behind the door. It sent chills throughout her body. Somehow she knew it was her step father, but never told anyone.

Some months later, Rita was at work where she had a casual conversation with one of the investigators, Lee. Through that conversation, they discovered they shared an interest in ghost hunting. Lee then shared with her that she belonged to the CTPS and invited her to join an upcoming investigation as a guest. It was a calming feeling to know she was around others who had gone through similar experiences as her. From there after, Rita became an active member of the team. Her belief is "when we leave our physical life, we never really go very far from the people or places that we love. Because of my new found belief, it has caused me to have a stronger interest in the paranormal world".

Jane - Field Investigator. Jane is the only member to join the team with no supernatural experiences in her past. Her path leading to the CTPS group was purely accidental. Having never experience a single paranormal incident in her entire life, she is the ideal representation of a true skeptic. It was at a chance meeting that would forever change her way of thinking.

One day while Jane was at her place of work, she was introduced to investigators, Lee and Rita. The two team members shared some of their paranormal experiences with her. Jane was captivated by their tales of seeing apparitions and even hearing the voices of ghosts. Sensing Jane's fascination, the members invited her to attend an investigation as a guest. With no hesitation, she quickly agreed. Since she's never seen a television ghost show or heard of anyone really seeing something supernatural first hand, it sounded interesting to her. Given she was a nonbeliever, she went into this agreement with little expectation. Unbeknownst to her, Jane was about to get a real wake up call.

Within a few weeks, the team got a call from a female client. She was having some minor, unexplainable activity in her home and it was causing her some concerns. The client worked out of her home and was growing tired of feeling a presence around her. Since it was nothing extraordinary and wanting to ease Jane into the world of paranormal research, they arranged for her to attend this simple investigation.

When the scheduled date arrived, the team put Jane right to work. There's no such thing as a guest when it comes to the CTPS. Everyone is required to pull their own weight during an investigation. Jane was stunned by how much is involved with the set up of the equipment. There were cameras, cables, tripods, extension cords, monitors, computers, voice recorders and even more cable, etc. She had no idea so much work went into the preparation just too possibly capture a glimpse of a ghost. Now that the set up was complete, a prayer was said and the investigation began. As the team lingers for the actual bewitching hour (2-4 AM), there's a lot of waiting, watching and quietness. During this time, Jane was becoming a little disenchanted. She was starting to think it was all for not. Then, suddenly the room grew full of activity and excitement. Lee called Jane over to the monitor and showed her something that would change her total thought process. Hanging in mid air by a cabinet door in the kitchen was a large, mist like figure. It was bright in color and free floating. Jane was bewildered. "How can this be? There are no such things as ghosts." or so she thought.

Now energized by this sighting, Jane wanted to be present at an

EVP session. The team led her inside and they took turns asking questions, even allowing Jane to ask a few. It went on for about an hour with no response. Returning to the command center, she was once again disillusioned since no ghost answered their questions. She watched as the team went over their recorded conversations word by word. Suddenly, Pop turned to her and smiled. He told her to listen carefully and keep an open mind. After a few seconds, you could hear Jane's gasp from across the room. A spirit had answered several of her questions. The revelation that ghost do exist can be frightening at first, especially if you've never questioned this before. Jane was no exception and was completely overwhelmed by it all.

As with most people who experience a paranormal occurrence, Jane now seeks her own answers. She has become a permanent CTPS member and has already attended numerous investigations. For Jane, she believes she is a better person from that chance meeting with the members. Her thoughts are "Although we can not see them, I have no doubt they exist. Despite the fact that we can't always hear them, they are out there and trying to communicate. As a CTPS investigator, I feel I can help us live in harmony with them. I believe, I believe, I believe and I love it."

Joey - The thing that most amazes the CTPS group about Joey, is how they came to know him. One day, he grew more curious about ghost hunting and sought out a paranormal group. Thankfully for everyone on the team, he discovered the web site of the CTPS. Using the form provided on-line, he applied as a volunteer investigator. Although the team receives volunteer request on a daily basis, this one caught their eye. Without any rational explanation, his application just stood out above the rest. His words were sincere, caring and for some reason gripping. The team was drawn to him by his likeability and they hadn't even met yet. After going over his application, they called him in for an interview.

As soon as they shook hands, they instantly knew Joey was to be a member of their team. What he conveyed in his application was exactly who he was, a good person. Joey is away fighting for our country right now. But his spot is being saved upon his return. Our thoughts and prayers are with him everyday he is away. It won't be much longer and we will have one of our favorite team members back . Before he left, we asked him to share his first paranormal encounter. This is what he said. The first occurrence that sparked Joey's fascination with the paranormal happened when he was around five years old. He had just been tucked in for the night and was drifting into a deep sleep. As he lay in his bed with all the lights off and the door closed, something suddenly woke him. As he rubbed his eyes to clear them, he was astonished by what he saw.

All around the room were what he described as "light people" walking in his walls. They were the complete opposite of what a shadow person would be thought of. These funny looking creatures were tall and incredibly bright. Each one had a different shaped head and were two dimensional having no depth. One of them had a head that was shaped like a half moon. He turned to see if there was a reflection coming from some outside source but there wasn't. The tallest one of them all started to come closer to Joey. Being only five years old and petrified, he turned over on his stomach hoping they would disappear. He could feel the tall "light man" standing over him. Joey bravely turned to look at the creature. As he looked up at the tall "light man" he could sense he was male. Unlike the others, he wasn't two dimensional. He then leaned out away from the wall and placed his hand on Joey's back. He could feel the touch. This was a bit much for such a young child. At that point, he got out of bed and ran to his Dad. Thinking it was just a nightmare, his Dad led him from room to room proving there was no one in the house. From then on, Joey has had countless unexplained things happen to him. Since that visit of the "light people", he has been intrigued by the supernatural and never sleeps with the lights off.

Chapter 7

The Lorena Saddle Club

The original CTPS group considers this to be their first genuine case. Although they tested out their new paranormal research tools in cemeteries and their own private homes it was just that, pure experimentation. As all new paranormal researchers discover, there are no "Ghost Hunting for Dummies" manuals or certified accredited schools on paranormal research. The only way to learn how to be a true investigator is by the school of hard knocks and without a doubt, the CTPS had their fair share.

By this time a few more team members had been added to the group. Each of them were just regular, hard working people searching for answers and validation for the paranormal things they had experienced in their past. Pop and Lee had acquired a minimal amount of equipment by now and the group was still getting a feel for conducting paranormal investigations. The lack of knowledge and experience didn't hold them back at all. If anything, they were more motivated than ever before. Looking back now, they wouldn't have changed a thing. The best way to learn something is by trial and error. For every investigation they landed on, the better they got. It's one thing to watch a show or hear other investigator's paranormal accounts but to see an apparition or shadow figure for the first time is breath taking. Each member had already witnessed something supernatural on these first few trial cases, now this new team was chomping at the bit to go find some ghost. Only thing was, how does one go about getting cases to investigate?

No sooner than Pop had asked himself this question, he was approached by a coworker wanting to confide in him about some abnormal activities occurring at her house. She explained that she been having a lot of odd things happening in her home. By now, Pop had received numerous false sightings by clients. Even though she was a coworker and he had known her for years, he was still a bit skeptical. Nevertheless, he gave her the benefit of the doubt and offered her his full attention. He could tell how sincere she was. She was actually quite shaken as she described the activity. She described seeing frightening shadow figures, objects moving on their own, and often hearing strange sounds which were like soft conversations coming from no where. After listening to her, he was convinced these sightings were

real. Considering the source and how her explanations sounded so legit plus the fact that the team was anxious to use their new equipment, Pop agreed to investigate her home. They decided the upcoming weekend was perfect.

The scheduled date had arrived and the team prepared to head out. They loaded up a couple of video cameras, a digital voice recorder and lots of coffee into Pop's truck. When they arrived they noticed the house was set back in a remote area next to an abandoned quarry. Not really having much of a plan, they just quickly dove into investigating. Being their first real investigation, there was an air of excitement. They began their EVP sessions and took lots of videos and still pictures. Although the evening resulted in really just a few orbs (which Pop is not yet convinced that these are really substantial evidence) being captured in still pictures, there was one significant piece of evidence seen. A shadow figure was caught on film moving between two members. It moved rapidly out of sync with the other movement on film. The team was ecstatic. Feeling they had made a legitimate find, they were more pumped than ever. Seeing how unorganized they felt that night, the team knew they needed better preparation going forward. This experience did the team wonders in motivating them causing them to become even more driven. Thankfully, another client approached them quickly. Except the team would had no idea how remarkable (almost life changing) this case was going to be for them.

This client contacted Pop to discuss some potential paranormal activity on his private property. The client was so nonchalant about the ghost sightings, Pop was some what leery. Then Pop could sense that the client was just confident that evidence would be found. Plus, he was familiar with the team's work and was actually friends with one of the team member's adult child. The client was so at ease with the paranormal activity seen throughout the building, he knew the team would have an exceptional investigation. Now growing more comfortable with the client, Pop attentively listened to the paranormal accounts of the client.

When Pop finally realized what building the client was offering them to research, he was enthralled. Pop and the team were raring to go for another case, but couldn't believe their stroke of luck. This client was offering them the opportunity to investigate the Lorena Saddle Club. The client explained that the building was located in the city of Lorena, Texas and had been used for riding events. The main building itself is old and dilapidated but was once used as a meeting place for a prominent local riding club. It had a riding arena with bleacher seating and bathroom facilities but no electricity available.

When Pop asked the client why the riding club stopped using the building for their events, he only stated "you'll see". The investigation date was arranged and the team couldn't wait for the day to arrive.

The team thought it would be helpful to do a historical background check on the property, so they decided to do some research. Now they've come to learn how imperative that is in an investigation. According to the public records and a colorful Lorena historian named "Boots", the building had been moved to the present location many years ago. It had once been a stagecoach depot, then a saloon and lastly a meeting place for the Saddle Club riders. This history sounded like a good combination for vast paranormal activity.

Feeling fairly well prepared, the investigation date had arrived and they were ready for what awaited them. As soon as the team gathered at Pop's house that evening, they quickly loaded up his truck with their small amount of equipment and headed for the Saddle Club. Being no electricity and no actual physical address, the place was rather hard to locate. Following the directions the client had given them, they made their way up a long dark gated road leading to the building. Everyone commented how dreary the atmosphere seemed. Oddly, the weather was pleasant and the moon full yet the air was thick and heavy. The team couldn't help but notice how strange it felt.

Using only their flashlights, they began to set up the equipment. The structure was a two story wood framed building with a lower level consisting of a main room, a kitchen area and a storage room. There were two doorways leading outside from the main room that was full of theater seats and a large desk. The desk was full of pictures dating back to the mid 1980's. The kitchen area had an old stove and empty cabinets that lined the walls. The back room had a sofa, mattresses and boxes of junk. After summing up the place, the team set up a digital video camera in the main room and kitchen area. Then they placed a digital voice recorder in the kitchen area and took digital pictures of everything. Completely uneasy in this building, they still tried to settle in for a long night.

With all the investigators sitting in the same room, they began their initial EVP session. No sooner than the first question asked, they could hear footsteps coming up the stairway. Looking all around to basically count heads making sure all the team members where counted for, they realized these were not the footsteps of any investigators. As the lead investigator took random still photos, she noticed every time she focused on the younger woman of the team, there would be a ghostly white mist hanging over her.

Their most moving image caught is what appears to be an apparition of a man walking down the stairway. With no more activity being noted, the team decided to call it a night. When they reviewed the tapes, they we're floored to hear their first Class "A" EVP. When one of the investigators asks a question you can easily hear a moan, then a voice saying "hello, talk to me".

With this new evidence and comprehending that with every investigation the team grows stronger in their ability, they set up another visit. This time the atmosphere was way more threatening. The investigators actually felt unwelcome and a feeling of dread. Many of the investigators were becoming uneasy. The team agreed not to stay very long and took numerous still photos. Again, whenever a still picture was taken of the younger investigator, there would be a ghostly white mist surrounding her. For most of the investigator's, the most disgusting part of this visit was the bugs which were everywhere. These weren't just mosquitoes or beetles, these were large Texas water bugs. It was like a scene from a horror movie. There were so many that you couldn't walk without stepping on them. As the team headed for Pop's truck and Lee's car, her vehicle lit up like an orange ball of flame. The team jumped into the car and drove off. Before leaving the Saddle Club, they had to stop and open the gate to leave the premises. When Lee got out of the car to open the gate, she turned and was flabbergasted. Bugs were crawling out of all her cars air vents. That visit certainly rank high on the weirdness meter for the investigators. Then once they reviewed the tapes when they got back home, all it did was make them want to visit again. The digital recorders had revealed numerous EVP's that night with female voices saying "find us", "hide" and "please help us" and a male voice that simple said "get out". Needless to say that visit gave the team the creeps, but not enough to stop them from going back.

Unbelievably, the team would return for a third and final time. This last visit would be described as almost surreal compared to the two previous ones. There were no feelings, no odd photos, and only one EVP. It seemed as though what ever had once been there was gone. The aura of the building felt flat almost dead. The team had used this building to help develop their investigation skills as well as discover all the incredible experiences they captured. Being grateful for this opportunity, the team decided to heed the spirit's last EVP which said "don't mess with this place". The team does not plan on returning in the future.

Chapter 8

Mosheim Mansion

Walking up to the Mosheim Mansion is like taking a step back in time. This gorgeous home was built in 1884 by Texas Governor, John Ireland. After losing the election for a second term, he sold it in 1894 to a local prominent attorney originally from Germany, named Emil Mosheim and his gorgeous Brazilian born wife, Lenora (Lena) Lowther. He and his wife raised their 10 children in this home. Sadly though, many of their children died in the home including, Emil and Lena themselves. After the couple passed away, the home was left to one of their daughters, Elsie. She lived out the remainder of her life in the home. After Elsie's passing, it changed hands numerous times. The present owners are now Carol & Bob Hirschi. This delightful couple transformed this mansion into a romantic Victorian Bed and Breakfast.

With the Mosheim family having lived there so long, the evidence found by the CTPS team surprised even them. As the CTPS group arrived at the mansion, they were greeted by two delightful women, Carol (the owner) and Lindsey (her assistant). Then several of the owner's adorable dogs came to say hello as well. The team has never had a more welcome greeting for an investigation. The whole experience felt as though they were visiting two long lost friends. As soon as the group stepped inside, they couldn't help but notice the furnishings of the mansion. The décor made you feel as though you had just entered a 1900's era steamship preparing to set sail on a voyage. There were beautiful antique dresses and gorgeous hats hung on seamstress forms resembling passengers arriving on board. The stairway made you feel as though the captain of the ship, Edward John Smith himself would be walking down any moment, it was dreamlike. Noticing the group's amazement, the owner quickly explained she was preparing the mansion for one of her annual dinner plays supporting several local organizations. The play's theme was to be "The Titanic". Carol had certainly done a stunning job because it felt just like that moment in time. One CTPS team member jokingly said "It feels so real, I want to go grab a life jacket just to be on the safe side"!

Carol suggested she'd give them a tour of the mansion to help become familiar with the building. Although no one could ever tell, the building is in reality two sections. The front area of the mansion facing the street is the original section of the building. The right side of the building has been added.

Whoever remodeled the building did an excellent job matching the bricks and windows. First Carol took them down into the basement by way of a tiny cast iron spiral staircase. This basement had been used as a wine cellar by the Mosheim family at one time. The beams, bricks and shelves of the original building were still intact and easily visible. Carol then walked the group through the entire house. Each room had been given a name such as Emma's Room, Marion's Room, the Grande Suite, The San Antonio and the Orleans. The newer section of the mansion had more modern facilities such as Jacuzzis and televisions yet retained that charming mood. The older section gave off a sense of history without even trying and is where the paranormal activity had been reported taking place. Carol explained what type of occurrences have been happening and where the hot spots were located. She was such a joy and an entertaining person, the team was in a sense of laughter the entire tour.

She described one experience how she would be walking into Emma's Room and could feel hard taps on the back of her head. She also described being pushed once in Marion's Room and seeing things disappear only to return later on without anyone being in the building. Every so often when her small dachshund would stand by the French doors, without any explanation the doors would open all by them selves, as if to let her in. The most annoying thing for Carol would be hearing her name called. She was forever answering it with no one there to respond to. Also, several guests have stated seeing a tall shadow figure glide past their door and an apparition of a woman wearing a large hat, sashaying down the hallway. With so much interesting activity described, the team was anxious to begin.

Having noted all the hot spots throughout the mansion, the team began to unload all of the equipment. Carol moves herself into the tiny maid's quarters next to the kitchen with all her pets and settles in for the night. Her room was above the wine cellar and the door that leads into the cellar was attached to her room. Since the team didn't want to bother her during the night, a camera was set up in the wine cellar but no live evp's would be performed there. The kitchen would now become the CTPS Command Center for the evening. There were doors that sectioned off the older building from the newer. It was the perfect arrangement for an investigation. Out of the kindness of her heart, Carol had offered the entire team free accommodations at the mansion for when the investigation was over. Astounded by her generosity, each member hurriedly selected their favorite room before the investigation started. Oddly, no one picked Emma's Room where most of the paranormal activity had been accounted.

The team decides to focus only on the original section of the mansion. Cameras are placed in each room and everything was secured in place. The set up and testing of the equipment goes quickly. By now its nightfall and Pop had given the go ahead to begin their investigation. Being around such a charming setting and having enjoyed the pleasant company of Carol and Lindsey so much, the team sensed nothing but easiness in the atmosphere. The aura of the house was so serene, they began to think this wasn't going to produce anything but a lovely evening for the group. The team would soon learn how fast things can change in just a matter of hours.

Before beginning the investigation, the team took numerous pictures and EMF readings of every room to use as a reference point. This is their normal routine procedure that is completed in case any changes are made in temperature or positions of furniture, paintings, etc. Then, the team walks around the outside perimeter of the house. This was done to orient the group of where the original building ended and the new addition began. As Pop looked up towards the third floor bedroom window, (which had originally been the attic now a bedroom) he saw something large slowly move. Needing to verify this, the team ran up there to inspect what that could have been. Upon reviewing the pictures just taken of the room, they noticed a mattress which had been set on its side by the window had fallen over. It had been leaning in such an angle it would have taken a great force to cause it to move to the other side. With this news, the team's expectations began to perk up.

Reverend Mark called everyone together and offered the team's protection prayer. He said "Although I don't think we're going to need it for this investigation, let's be on the safe side" and everyone agreed. The first team of investigators went into the older section to begin their EVP session. The interior of the home is so exquisitely decorated with antiques and quality furnishings, it's like walking around a museum. There's so much to look at and it would be easy to be distracted.

The investigation team stayed inside about an hour or so and nothing was captured at that time. Then another team of investigators went in and also stayed for over an hour. You can tell by the team's digital recordings, they were certain there's nothing to capture in this mansion in the way of paranormal evidence. Their EVP sessions turned more casual conversations with each other instead of focusing on the research. You could tell by the team's recordings they were enjoying the mansion more than the research. When the team wasn't in the older section conducting EVP sessions, they were mainly discussing the incredible beauty and history of the mansion. Carol had provided a huge binder full of information and pictures on the mansion's history for the team to flip through. Everyone took turns reading it. The mansion's history is amazing.

By now it's almost 3:00 AM. Two investigators, Dana and Shelley and their invited guest, Erin were conducting the last EVP session in the gentlemen's smoking parlor. Still believing there was no paranormal activity in this building, they followed through with the final questioning. Then suddenly, Shelley felt an ice cold breeze on the right side of her body as if someone had raced past her. She stated something had just touched her leg. Then, Erin felt the exact experience on her left side as though something had passed between them. At that same moment, there was a loud thump drawing Dana's eyes towards the back window. The window was located behind Shelley and Erin. When Dana looked in that direction she saw a tall, thin shadow figure dash across the room. Completely stunned that activity was actually happening, both Shelley and Dana reached for their walkie talkies to contact command center hoping they caught it on video. The investigators called Pop several times with no reply. Although Pop could see them in the video, he had no idea something had just happened. When the investigators didn't receive a response, Shelley left the room to report to the command center in person. When she returned to the team waiting in the smoking room, she surprisingly explained all of the newly charged batteries in the walkie talkies had been drained of power during their session. Upon reviewing their video, sadly the shadow figure had been positioned in an area the camera couldn't capture it.

Unshaken and totally excited now by the episode, the team of three (with fully charged walkie talkies again), headed upstairs to the room called Marion's Suite. This room was actually two rooms with an enormous wooden sliding door to separate the two areas. It was once used as a nursery and nanny's room by the Mosheim family. As the team began their EVP session once again, they laid a K-2 meter on the table. Each team member asked a question hoping for a response. For some reason, the K-2 meter would light up only when Erin would ask something. It registered all the way to the top numerous times. After about 30 minutes of questioning, the room became engulfed with the aroma of gardenias. They couldn't figure out where it was coming from. It was the middle of winter and gardenias aren't in bloom then. Considering the strong readings happened every time Erin asked a question, Dana encouraged her to continue. Not being an investigator, she was somewhat hesitant but agreed. Her next question would be if any of the

Mosheim Family members were present in the room. The K-2 meter then hit the top range again and held its position. Once completed with the EVP session, the team thanked the spirits for letting them visit and started to leave the room. Dana led the way down the stairs, followed by Shelley. Erin (who normally stays between two investigators at all times) was still at the top of the stairs turning off the video camera she had been holding. As Erin took the first step on the stairs leading downward an eerie, ice cold feeling began to fill the atmosphere around her. Then, she heard a male's voice softly whisper "turn around". Knowing the two investigators she was with were female and she could even see them directly in front of her, she was confused by hearing a male's voice. She then stopped instantly in her tracks. When she turned to look towards Marion's suite as the voice had requested her to, the air above her began to swirl with energy. The hair on her arms was standing straight up. The temperature of the second floor had dropped drastically and was freezing. Without a doubt Erin was frightened and quietly called to the investigators to wait as she took a few steps down the stairs. Just then, she could feel something touching her back. It was as if someone had lightly rested their hands on her shoulder blades with a gentle yet electrically charged contact. She was so alarmed by this, she ran to catch up with the investigators. However, the feeling wouldn't stop as if it had a hold of her. Realizing Erin was having a physical encounter with a spirit, Shelley told the ghost in an assertive voice to "please stop, you're scaring her". In a blink of an eye, everything stopped. The room became warm, the atmosphere was no longer electrically charged and the feeling on her back was slowly fading away. By now, Pop and Reverend Mark could see in the video that something was wrong. In the quick time the team was halfway out the area, both men were by their side.

Pop asked Erin if she was alright now. She reassured him that she could still feel the tingling in her back, but everything was okay. Hating to end the investigation with such high activity being generated, daylight was gaining upon them. The team quickly headed to there rooms to catch at least a few hours sleep before heading back home.

The team got in about four hours of sleep, then got up to collect the equipment. Carol was now wide awake and offering everyone coffee. She was curious to know if the team had captured any evidence or felt anything. They all looked at each other and giggled softly. Carol figured they'd tell her sooner or later and let it go. The team thanked Carol and Lindsey for their hospitality and promised to send them the results of the investigation once everything had been reviewed. The team members returned back to their homes feeling good about the investigation. Throughout the next couple of

days, Pop and the team reviewed the EVP's. He reviewed the section where the investigator saw the shadow figure in the smoking room. Unbelievably, you can hear a voice speaking several sentences in some sort of foreign language. It's very lengthy. The team has yet to be able to translate it. Then, when Pop got to the section where Erin says "I'd like to know if anyone here is a member of the Mosheim family", Pop could easily hear an answer of a deep, male voice stating "No"! After the strange incident, he wasn't sure Erin would really want to hear the response. He decided to send it to her by e-mail letting her make the decision on her own. Surprisingly, she was thrilled to hear it. She said the evidence made her realize she hadn't imagined it. When asked about the experience, she admitted being frightened by the encounter. Yet looking back, she wished she could have remained calmer and waited to see what the spirit wanted. The touch was so gentle, she felt he just wasn't ready for her to leave yet. She felt that maybe he wanted to tell her who he was but wasn't given enough time to do it.

The CTPS team was grateful for Carol and Lindsey allowing them to investigate the mansion. Beside meeting two very nice ladies, staying the night in a gorgeous mansion and meeting some wonderful dogs, the paranormal evidence that was captured at the Mosheim Mansion was beyond memorable. The team can not wait to return for another investigation and hopes to attend the next Mosheim Mansions' "Titanic" dinner play event!

Chapter 9

Copperas Cove

This is the home that resulted in one of the most haunting EVP's the CTPS team ever captured. It was revealed in the Command Center right after it was caught as an invited guest listened in. Knowing this would be the first EVP the guest has ever heard, made it even more exciting to share. For the investigators, watching someone hear their first EVP is a sight to be seen. It's like watching a child's first glimpse of Santa Claus, amazed yet somewhat afraid. The team has witnessed responses of uncontrollable laughter to near fainting spells. It's always an enjoyable experience for the team to be able to share their captured evidence, especially with first timers. This guest gave the team the most memorable and hilarious reaction ever. It's one of the team's favorite stories to share.

First, here's a little behind the CTPS scenes note for you. When most paranormal groups (and especially the CTPS members) speak about previous investigation cases, they will take something that stood out about the case to nickname it as their reference. This is done because many of their clients are private homes and wish to remain anonymous. Nicknaming the investigation case help's maintained the client's privacy but allows the team to openly discuss the case amongst them. A good example would be the house in Penelope, Texas. It is called "the most disturbing house" instead of the client's name, town or the physical address. For the Copperas Cove, it is named after the incredible class "A" EVP which they captured. Even though the team was certain they'd obtain some evidence from this home, they never expected the quality in which it was received.

When the Copperas Cove client sent in the completed on-line investigation request form, it was rather short. The client was vague about the paranormal accounts he was having. Yet, Pop (who has a very keen intuition when it comes to people) had a gut feeling this client was in fact sincere. He then contacted the client to verify that it was a valid request for help. They spoke briefly on the phone and Pop could sense something was up. There was a hint of urgency in the client's voice. The client kept stating how the paranormal activity was concerning his son. Once everything sounded authentic and in order, a personal visit by several team members would be the next step. A meeting was arranged at the house the very next day. It would be Pop and Reverend Mark who would make the trip there. As they arrived at

the house, they couldn't help but notice a sense of sorrow to the home. It was as if the house had an aura of sadness to it. Having grown familiar with these immediate feelings of dread, the team of two knew this wasn't going to have a pleasant outcome.

They were greeted by an older man and his extremely quiet adult son. Knowing that there were two men living there, the team expected the house to be full of stuff. Only to discover, the house was almost empty. It had a couple televisions, chairs and lots of video games but very little furniture. The client quickly explained that the home wasn't their primary resident. It was their weekend home used mainly as a "man cave" type place for the guys to hang out. The client went on to say that although they didn't live there full time, the annoyance of the paranormal activity was troubling his son. They were hoping the CTPS would be able to remove what ever it was causing the disturbances. After the team did a walk through, they all sat down to begin the interview. They placed several EMF meters on the table in front of them. No sooner than the team took a seat, all EMF meters registered to the fullest point.

Needless to say, the interview didn't take long at all.

Seeing the EMF meters flaring up throughout the entire conversation offered some strong paranormal activity at hand. Pop and Reverend Mark still went through the process of asking where the hot spots were and what had been seen to follow the normal procedure. The client acknowledged there had been black masses and shadow like figures seen throughout the house. For some reason they were more prominent in the back bedroom. Plus, the constant doors slamming on there own were becoming upsetting. This was enough for Pop and Mark to agree to help the client out. They also felt there was an immediate need for help, so the investigation was scheduled for the next weekend. The team reassured the client they would do everything in their power to help and headed back to their base headquarters.

Pop then contacted their team historian and made a request for a historical background check of the house. Being the investigation was in just a few days, she got right on it. As she began to go over the lengthy data of the house's history, mind-boggling information began to surface. She was completely taken back with her discovery! This gloomy feeling small house definitely had some large deep, dark secrets tucked away. Astonishingly it didn't have just one secret, it had two.

The historian had unexpectedly uncovered that two separate violent murders had occurred in the house. Sadly, the deaths had been inflicted in a very brutal manner. Shocked by her findings, she sent the gruesome information to the team and wished them luck. The team already knew it was going to be an unpleasant investigation but this new found information made them uneasy. All they could do was hope for the best and prepare for the worse. On the day of the scheduled investigation, the preparation went as smooth as usual. The clients had made arrangements to sleep elsewhere being they are not allowed to be present during the investigation. They let the team into the home and said their goodbyes. Set up began and things were put into place quickly. One of the team member's had an adult child visiting from another city, so she was invited to attend the investigation. To experience the investigation to the fullest, the guest was put straight to work. It's always entertaining to watch a guest's face when Pop tells them paranormal investigating isn't a spectator sport, so get to work. For the most part, CTPS guest enjoy being "hands on" more than just sitting around watching. It gives the guest a true feeling of what it's like to do paranormal research. Without hesitation, the guest dove right in.

With everything in place, Reverend Mark says the team's protection prayers then all the lights are turned off. Pop never allows an investigator to enter a building being researched alone. For the team's safety, they must be accompanied by another team member at all times. Teams of two enter the house taking turns lasting around an hour each. Monitoring of the team is constant by way of videos and two way radios in the Command Center. Like most investigations, it starts off slow. Except that some of the female investigators kept feeling something like cobwebs moving across their face from time to time, the activity was minimal. As the evening makes its way into the early morning hours, the paranormal activity gradually begins to escalate. EMF meters begin to fluctuate at high registers and members are experiencing physical touching of the hair. The team leader captures a bright mist floating in the air and loud banging sounds in rooms that were completely empty. Numerous EVP sessions were conducted and were being reviewed throughout the night as teams would turn them in. As a surprise to their guest, she was allowed to enter the house to be a part of the investigations. Although hesitant at first, she agreed. Accompanying her mother who is a skilled investigator, they made their way into the back bedroom where most of the activity was occurring. Being an older house, each step they took caused the wooden floors to make noises. In the taped conversation between the guest and her mother, you can hear them mention this in the recording. The daughter states how the floors sure creek a lot and the mother replies how it's worse in the front living room. They remained for a good hour or so but nothing was observed or felt. Returning to the Command Center where the analysis team was waiting to review there EVP recordings, they handed them over and a team member starts to review it. By now the activity had tapered off and they were about to call it a night. The team begins to pick up the equipment when the lead analysis investigator makes a rather loud gasp. As everyone turns to look at her, she slowly lays her headset down as though puzzled and looks at the guest. Then she smiled and asked the guest if she could handle something rather intense. The guest said "of course, yes", then questioned her as to why. The analysis investigator told her to be prepared and placed the headset over her ears. As soon as they pressed played and pointed out where the EVP section could be heard using the wavepad on the monitor, the guest eyes grew larger and larger. The EVP was then looped to make certain she got the whole effect. Unexpectedly, the guest took the headset off her head, threw them across the room and made a comment the team never expected. Unfortunately, we're unable to repeat what she said. It was so hilarious, the team was in tears from laughter. Even though she was frigthened at first, she wanted to listen to it over and over. When the two ladies had been inside asking questions during the EVP session, you can distinctly hear a Class "A" response of a man saying "BRING ME HOME!"

Thinking this was all the team was going to get, they began loading up. After everything was packed up and ready to go, two team members went back in for a walk through making sure everything was as they found it. As they began to walk out the house, one of the team members turned to thank the spirits for allowing them to visit. It's a practice most paranormal investigators follow. Knowing the house was in order and empty, the members turn to lock the door behind them. Without any explanation, the handle to the toilet began to jiggle numerous times as if someone was trying to reset the tank and it began to flush all on its own. They raced back into the house to make sure nothing was wrong with the tank or plumbing. This hadn't happen at all during the course of the investigation, not even once. Their conclusion was this was the spirits last chance at getting their attention. Since it takes little effort to receive big results by pushing a toilet handle, this is something seen in many investigations. The members again thanked the spirits and returned to their homes.

After the full analysis of the investigation had been completed, the team agreed the spirits there mean no harm. Even though there had been two horrific acts of violence in the house, the overall aura was sad but the spirits were harmless. The client was advised of this and has chosen to coexist with the ghost. The CTPS had made him realize there was no real danger living there. All that was needed was for the client to take control of his home and things should improve. Oddly, there have been no more occurrences at the house. The father and son have been enjoying their quality time once again. Though the guest who heard her first EVP was somewhat shaken, she is now one of the CTPS team's biggest fans and hopes to return again for another investigation.

Chapter 10

Central Texas Hospital

Over the summer of 2010, the CTPS was given permission to conduct an investigation at a hospital that had recently been vacated. The team had wanted to investigate this building for a long time since the history of this place was so incredible. It had been built in the late 1800's and had seen a vast amount of suffering within the walls. With so much history passing, the paranormal accounts experienced by the medical staff were numerous. For most of the employees, they had become accustomed to the ghostly activities. Those that had grown tired of the haunts were glad to be moving to another facility. Now that it was a completely empty building, it was the perfect opportunity to hold an investigation. Unbelievably, the administration of this hospital agreed to let the CTPS be the group to investigate it. Just about every Texas ghost hunting group wanted to research this historical place. As you can imagine, the team members were ecstatic to be chosen for this event.

Since the building was so huge, it would require the full CTPS team and all their part time volunteers to achieve a thorough investigation. They were also fortunate enough to recruit the founder of the renowned G.H.O.S.T. Paranormal Group to help cover this massive building.

With much anticipation, the night of the investigation had finally arrived. Before setting up, they were given a tour of the facility by one of the security officers, named Chris. He gave the team an enormous amount of history of the hospital and even shared some of his own personal ghost experiences he had encountered while working there.

Then the daunting task of setting up the equipment came. The group used every piece of equipment they owned. There were IR cameras down hallways and in patient rooms. Lasers and motion sensors were set up everywhere in hopes of capturing evidence of the many apparitions claimed to have been seen by the hospital staff members. After several hours of exhausting work, the group was ready to begin. They broke into teams of two, with everyone stationed in a certain area. They were to remain in that area so that the evidence would not be contaminated by other members. Each team then began sweeping the hospital for signs of any paranormal activity.

With such a large group of investigators, every inch of that building was being scrutinized. From the furnace room in the basement to the meeting rooms on the top floor, the team left no stone unturned. As one might imagine there were many personal experiences had by almost everyone that night.

One team had headed down into the furnace room to conduct an EVP session. Every time a question was asked out loud, the pipes would make a groaning sound in perfect order to the questions. The team even challenged this several times to make certain it wasn't a coincidence. They would ask questions slower then faster and with each question, the answers came right after being asked.

Their newest team member at the time was with a group of four who were investigating the children's ward. She was startled by a cold sensation on the back of her neck and then the chain of her necklace was slowly lifted. The first physical contact from a spirit is always alarming, so she was without a doubt shaken by the event. All of the team members would hear shuffling of papers and the clinking of keys throughout the floor. The most unusual event for the group was the gentle laughter of children off in the distant. It wasn't frightening though, it was more of a comforting feeling.

According to Chris (the security guard), the seventh floor had the most paranormal occurrences reported in the entire hospital. This was the level of the ICU department. Two of the male CTPS' experienced team members decided to tackle this area. There was one certain room that seemed to be particularly active. The security guard recalled how the staff members would constantly contact him concerning this room. They would report an unknown man was seen in that specific room that kept waking up the patients. Every time he'd check it out, no one would be there. One of the most interesting accounts would come from the housekeeping staff. Every morning they would come in to clean the room and the bible would be lying on the bed. It would always be opened to the same passage without fail.

Fascinated by all these paranormal accounts described by Chris, the two male investigators couldn't wait to begin their EVP session on this level. When they exited the elevator, they sat down in an area that was located in the middle of the corridor. No sooner than they had turned on the digital recorder, they could hear soft music playing in the background. As the two investigators searched for the source of the tune, they called to the command center to see if maybe someone had a radio on. Before the command center techs could answer, they realized it was coming from one of the rooms down the hallway. Hurriedly they headed towards the room and as soon as they got close to the source it stopped. Knowing the chances that this event was captured on the recorder, they promptly hit the rewind button. Sure enough, off in the distance soft music could be heard playing very faintly. Several days later, this haunting event would be validated by a female nurse who use to work in the ICU at the hospital. During a casual conversation with this nurse about the investigation, she told a CTPS member the most heartfelt story. She remembered a particular female patient who laid in ICU unconscious for weeks. Recognizing the patient was taking a turn for the worse, the spouse was informed by this nurse. He couldn't bear to live without her, so he attempted to save her life the only way he could think of. He brought in a record player and played their favorite song together over and over. He had hoped that maybe she would recognize it and wake up. Unfortunately, she never recovered. It was that room that the spouse had lost his sweetheart. The investigators believe this was her favorite song being played once again.

    The biggest find during this long night of investigating actually wouldn't be revealed until days later. It wasn't until after the analysis team was going over the evidence that the team would learn of this incredible find. Chris was escorting the two male investigators into one of the operating suites. Several claims of paranormal activity had been reported in this room. The previous staff members stated they could hear footsteps walking back and forth as if there was someone pacing. Bottles in the cabinet were heard being moved about and the list goes on and on. Hoping to at least capture an EVP, the men begin wandering around the room ready to begin their questioning. Neither one of them had a clue that a full apparition had walked right in front of them. The video secured is of a male figure wearing what the CTPS group believes to be a Civil War soldier's uniform. The most amazing thing that makes this video so noteworthy is the location. The apparition is seen inside a glassed in closest. There is no way in or out but through the doors that the camera is aimed at. As the figure reveals him self, he enters through one wall and exits through another. The team had no idea this spirit had been watching their every move.

    Needless to say, the entire CTPS group was surprised by this incredible piece of supernatural proof. This investigation had produced dozen's of EVPs and physical contacts by ghosts. These alone were significant pieces of evidence. But to have a disembodied spirit manifest its self right in front of the investigators path is remarkable. The video is a jaw dropping, mind boggling experience. It has been shown to paranormal investigators around the state of Texas and is ranked as one of the most compelling pieces of paranormal evidence.

    For the CTPS group, this investigation was their most exciting and rewarding. They (as dozens of other groups) had wanted to explore behind the hospital's doors for years. In their opinion, the wait was definitely worth it. It was an extraordinary experience for every investigator that was present that evening. Oddly enough, the hospital wasn't torn down after it was vacated. The building was sold and a new owner has developed the property. The team has often wondered if the new occupants ever notice a strange man in their room, soft music playing in the background or a Civil World soldier walking their the hallways?

Chapter 11

Lorena, Texas (Private Home)

This investigation yielded the team's second most compelling videos ever captured. Although nothing substantial was even revealed through still photos or digital recordings, the video evidence was enough to want to share this investigation. A full clip can be viewed on the CTPS web site.

The team decided to take this case because children were involved. Since most of the investigator's are parents, hearing children were being exposed to the paranormal activity tugged at their heart strings. This on-line request for an investigation was made by a young couple from Lorena, Texas. They had lived in the house for over four years and had never experience anything peculiar. Then unexpectedly, the family started to notice odd things happening around the home. With their children ranging from ages 21 months to 12 years old, anyone would expect the house to be filled with the typical lively noises and playful commotion. Here lately though, certain events just weren't adding up as normal.

It began with the family experiencing unusual interference with their electronic devices throughout the house. Even after having their house checked for electrical problems, things would continue to turn on and off for no reason. This was more annoying than anything. Then one of their children could be heard almost every night having long conversations with someone while she slept. When the child would wake up, she would describe a red headed older lady she had dreamt about. For the parents, this was disturbing because an apparition of an elderly woman with red hair had been seen moving from room to room. There were no claims of harm being done but as any parent would be, they were growing concerned for their children.

Before the scheduled investigation date, the team historian had fully researched the property. It was discovered that the original home for this location had been torn down and removed for unknown reasons. The present home had been moved there and recently renovated. After interviewing the neighbors, they stated that a red haired woman had actually been the original owner of the house that had been demolished. Having this information did confirm the sighting, and it increased the possibility of discovering more details.

When the scheduled date arrived, the team showed up just after dark to meet with the family and discuss their concerns of paranormal activity. After a brief tour of the home, base line readings of EMF, temperature and humidity were performed. IR cameras were set up to document the two long hallways within the home and in the children's rooms. As usual, they divided into teams of two to take pictures, videos and attempt EVP sessions.

While conducting an EVP session in the master bedroom, one of the investigators started feeling peculiar and had a strange look about her. The other team member could tell she just didn't seem like her usual self. She became quiet and detached, which was way out of the norm for her. Whispering to her team member, she asked if they could leave because she wasn't comfortable in the house. As the two investigators began to leave the room, a black mass resembling a person was seen making its way down the hallway. Startled by the shadow figure and her increasingly odd feelings, the investigator needed to get out of the house. In her eyes, the sooner the better. They stepped outside to get some fresh air and within minutes, she was back to herself again. When asked what had happened, she was unable to fully explain it. She could best describe the feeling as an out of body experience, as if in a hypnotic state. A new team took over as she and her partner remained in the Mobile Command Center for awhile. It was later discovered that the shadow figure had been captured in a still photograph. Another photograph revealed a bright white mist amongst a pile of stuffed toy animals right next to where the investigator had been sitting.

The next group of investigators headed into the back bedroom where the activity had been most significant. This was the bedroom that belonged to the two younger boys. As one would expect, there was an assortment of toys, books, video games and comic book character posters all about the bedroom. On top of one of the bookshelves there were numerous electronic toys lined up. These toys were somewhat dusty indicating they had not been played with for some time. During the teams EVP session in this room, a mechanical sounding noise was heard in the kitchen area. They stopped the EVP session to check out the noise. It was discovered to be a clock that made tractor sounds on the hour, but for some reason it had gone off before it was suppose to. All the time they were in the kitchen, they could hear mechanical noises coming from the rooms they had just left. It was as though someone was playing a game with them. When they hurried to return, they were stunned to see one of the battery operated toys blaring its lights and sounds uncontrollably. It was a large toy dinosaur. Thinking the batteries would sooner or later wear out, they let it continue. The toy wildly screamed, roared and lit up for nearly five minutes. Finally one of the investigators took it off the shelf to remove the batteries when the dinosaur immediately stopped. She examined the toy to see if maybe it had a short or crossed wire and didn't find anything. To guarantee that the toy would not interrupt their EVP session again, she attempted to remove the batteries from it. When she opened the back of the toy, she was shocked to learn the dinosaur's battery compartment was completely empty. The toy never had batteries in it to begin with. Where it got its energy from was a mystery to the entire team.

Although the rest of the Lorena investigation was uneventful, the team feels they captured some stunning evidence. Their analysis of the case is that the spirit haunting was simply playful and looking for attention. Pop and the investigator's suggested learning to coexist with the spirit yet set rules which the spirit must follow. By taking control of the house, harmony can be maintained within the home. As with any long term guest, setting boundaries help make for a more pleasant stay. The owner's took CTPS' advice and the team was never called back.

Chapter 12

Penelope, Texas (Private Home)

This case has been deemed the CTPS's "most disturbing home". They have had to return to the property several times and the massive paranormal activity still lingers. CTPS has yet to resolve this client's paranormal issues but they have vowed to not give up.

The introduction to this female client was obtained by the usual method. The client filled out the on-line investigation request form explaining how she and her adult children were being terrified by something unexplainable. Once Pop received and reviewed the form, he didn't hesitate at all moving forward with this investigation. He knew the team was going to take on this case just from the client's explanation. The woman's paranormal experiences were so ghastly and numerous, Pop had a gut feeling about this case. His intuition is usually accurate when it comes to people. This client would prove Pop to once again be correct in his insight.

Without hesitation or even interviewing the client, he immediately turned the case over to the research department. Wanting to be prepared before entering this building, he believed knowing the history of this property would certainly give him an advantage while conducting the interview. He waited until he had the historical results before setting up the personal consultation. Understanding Pop's concerns, the research team got right on it.

As the team began to explore this property's past, they learned it wasn't just the client's building itself that was unique. The history of the area the building was located in was even more note worthy. The entire town had a very colorful past and was full of interesting facts. CTPS's team members contacted some of the neighbors and local citizens for more firsthand information. During their discussions, the team learned that dozens of ghost sightings had been registered in this town. The numerous energy and paranormal activities are overwhelmingly strong throughout this quaint but mystifying little corner of the world. The ghost descriptions told by the residents (mostly descendants of the original settlers) who live here are sufficient enough to make anyone think twice about spending the night in this town. The whole town of Penelope, Texas could be described as a genuine "Ghost Town". The local's encounters made the team want to investigate every building in this small town. With so much rich history being shared, the team's research went way beyond just the clients' property. They discovered the first settlers in this area where the wealthy Seley Family who in 1890 established a large ranch. It was called the Zee Vee Ranch. Then in 1902 the International-Great Northern Railroad arrived and initiated the purchase of land beside the tracks. This helped create the town and was then named after Penelope Trice who was the daughter of the railroad's president. Numerous Czech families moved into the region and Penelope was soon established as a shipping and market center for farmers and ranchers. The town became known for its spectacular black-prairie cotton. It was once a booming community. Many artifacts can actually still be found from its cotton producing heyday. The town's pride and joy are the two old cotton scales. By 1920 the town had an estimated population of four hundred and twenty businesses. This included a bank, three large cotton gins, a lumber company, a newspaper, several churches, a school and even a resident doctor. Back then that was a rare commodity for the towns people as most of the residents were still farmers. Penelope declined as a result of the Great Depression, World War II and the construction of highways that made the job opportunities in nearby Dallas and Waco more attractive. The population was listed as two hundred in 2000 and only two businesses. Today, Penelope is basically a ghost town.

The client's small house and another building (which was once used as a church for the town) was initially owned by one of the original Czech families that migrated to Penelope. Although the house and church had been moved from its original location (next to a cemetery) to where it is now, the ownership of the buildings has been maintained by descendants of the original founders of the Penelope town.

The team's client was the grand daughter of one of these descendants. Her grandfather had recently passed away. She had moved into the home with several of her children and numerous pets. No sooner than she had moved in, the paranormal sightings began.

When the investigation date had arrived, the team met early and was then briefed about what the client had claimed to have seen. As Pop read over the list of sightings, the amount was so large one of the investigator's said "wouldn't it be easier to just state what hasn't been seen here instead"?

Knowing this case was going to produce a lot of evidence, the team arranged for cameras, videos and digital recorders in almost every room. They were ready for the worst. When the team was given the go ahead, the first group went in. That evening the weather was unbearably hot and they were using the Mobile Command Center (MCC) to monitor this event. Since the MCC did not have air conditioning at this time, this meant it was going to be one long uncomfortable night.

For their first stop, the team would investigate the building that was once used as a church. It was rather difficult to maneuver around the area because the old church was now used as a storage facility. One of the investigators noticed a large hole in the floor that had been damaged by neglect and led to the underground area below. Oddly the temperature in the church was miserably hot, yet the air coming from the open area below was freezing cold. With no electricity in this building, they knew it wasn't from any air conditioning ducts. Suddenly, the investigators all began to have a deep sense of apprehension about them. It was as if the atmosphere had changed from a gentle feeling to an unmistakably tense aura. One of the investigators' whispered "this is one sad place". Continuing with the investigation, they moved into the small house next door.

The overall mood of the house was described by one of the investigator's as purely depressing. The client's pet had just given birth to a large litter of puppies. The investigators noted that even the animals looked gloomy. It was the most unpleasant feeling the team has ever felt from inside a home.

The team headed into the very back room where most of the activity had occurred. No sooner than one of the investigators stepped into the room, she felt an icy hand abruptly grab her leg. The sensation was remarkably cold and prickly. She was startled by this extraordinary physical contact but decided to continue with the EVP session. The activity was way to strong to quit and she refused to leave. With nothing else noted after a while, they moved the investigation into the next room (this was the master bedroom). The room had a peculiar feeling to it but the team just couldn't put their finger on it. It was as if there was someone else in the room with them, like they weren't alone. The team started walking out of the room and back through a hallway, at that moment the investigators could hear loud gasps coming from inside the command center. The team contacted them on their walkie talkie and asked if everyone was alright. Pop said "ya'll might want to come take a look at this".

The team made their way outside to the MCC and questioned Pop as to what was going on. They could tell everyone was excited about something. While the tech manager was rewinding the video back to where the team was just leaving the master bedroom, he was grinning the whole time. Then Pop said "tell me if you notice anything?" As everyone looked on, the two investigators' could clearly see that a shadow figure had stepped right in front of one of them. She had almost been nose to nose to it. The figure then turns and heads directly into the camera. After this sighting, the investigator decides it was a bit much to take in and asked for a short break. It was agreed by everyone, that a new team of investigators should now go in. They soon found out, the spirits were ready to be heard more than seen now. Knocks were being heard everywhere. When they asked the spirit

to react to the well-known "shave and a hair cut two bits" knock, the team got a response every time. Numerous and upsetting EVPs were captured and recorded. By now, it was almost daylight and it was time to bring the investigation to a close.

Pop told the client the buildings were indeed haunted and his best advice would be to take control of her home. He believed she needed to let the spirits know that she lived in this home not them and that they are just guest. He taught her how to continue this practice until CTPS could come back and Reverend Mark said some prayers. She agreed and the group left expecting to return soon.

Several weeks passed and just as they had promised, the team made another visit to the home. The client said that things hadn't been as aggressive as it was in the past but that odd things were still happening. The house looked different to the team, as if some remodeling had begun. For the team, there was an over all change to the place. It felt less threatening.

The group set up all the equipment once again and they began their investigation. All of the members agreed that the atmosphere was far less menacing this time. The client stated she had been continuing with her aggressive demands for the spirits to follow her rules. It was obvious the approach was working. This time nothing was caught on video but the spirits were anxious to speak their mind. Several EVP's were captured and not to pleasant at that.

One EVP caught was a class "a" female voice saying "Get Out!", then a male voice saying the same thing. When an investigator asked if some one was present, a voice can be heard saying "Pat". Pop approached the client to ask if she had known someone named Pat. Her face became suddenly pale and it was apparent she had definitely known this person. She explained that was her aunt's name that recently passed away. She had once lived in the house. It was noted that right where the EVP had been captured, the team had been standing next to a stuffed teddy bear doll that had once belonged to her Aunt Pat.

Sensing the house had far less activity than the previous time, the group's consciences were that their advice had been working. Since the spirits were not harmful or hostile, it was agreed by everyone that there was no need to rid the spirits. As long as the client was growing more comfortable with their existence, the team felt it would be possible for them to cohabitate with one another.

The client is still having paranormal occurrences around the home but has learned to live with it. She contacts the CTPS mostly for moral support which that are glad to give her.

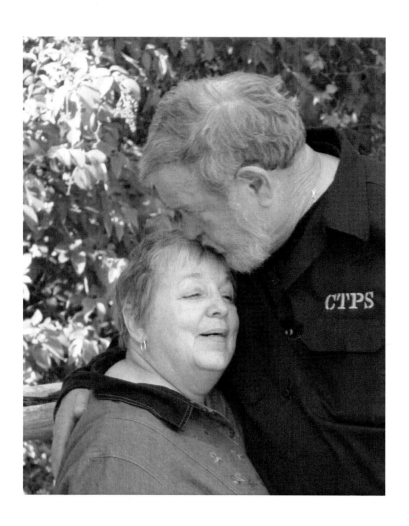

Chapter 13

Authors Conclusion

I purposely saved the conclusion of this book until my journey with the CTPS group was one hundred percent complete. For me it was important that I have a genuine understanding of the group once I had reached this point. Although writing this book was a personal goal, I also wanted it to be a learning experience. The goal wasn't to simply write a biography about a unique group of paranormal investigators. My intentions were to also learn more about something I wasn't quite convinced existed. In the short months it's taken me to carry out this task, I feel as though I have accumulated a wealth of knowledge. I believe I can walk away from this experience knowing I achieved my objective.

When I began writing this book, I and the members of the CTPS group were complete strangers (except for my sister, Shelley who was already a member). With each investigation, every one talking about their clients, the photo shoot, the numerous phone conversations and e-mails back and forth, I grew increasing closer to them. Now, they are no longer just a paranormal group to me, they are my friends. Must admit, I didn't anticipate this. I came into this project with an invisible force field around me, prepared not to let these people get into my heart. I had convinced myself that I had no intention of growing close to them. Just get the book written and be done. I sum that attitude up to mostly my fear of the unknown. This group of people explored things that frightened me and I didn't want to get caught up in it.

There is no way someone could meet the CTPS team and walk away without feeling that you have just come in contact with a special group of people. What you didn't read in their bios is how hard working these individuals are. They live regular daily lives with their family and friends. Yet they put in long hours of unpaid work just to gather more evidence on the paranormal phenomenon. This unique group of people are sincerely in it to help.

My favorite part about the group is the laughter. With all the tedious work they put into an investigation, there's always room for pleasant chitchat. Listening to Pop and Lee's lighthearted teasing with one another, Reverend Mark's jokes and Dana's gentle way made a serious event

actually fun. Something else I didn't count on was developing a stronger conviction that ghost are real. This is so out of the norm for me. I've always been comfortable with my religious beliefs. I never feared death because I was content in how I saw the afterlife. Being around the CTPS group, hearing their experiences and going on an investigation with them caused me to question my theory. I developed a sense of confusion. My thought process never included spirits being left behind. That didn't fit in with my way of thinking when it came to my faith. Though I must admit now, ghosts do exist. They are definitely amongst us and I've experienced it first hand.

It's one thing to hear about it from another or see it on a television show. When you come in contact with something supernatural for yourself, it changes you whole way of thinking. I'm not exaggerating when I tell you that I have seen, heard and felt their presence personally. The first time you here a spirit speak, it changes you. The first EVP I ever heard was a male voice saying "Bring me home". It nearly broke my heart. I see now why the team is so somber when they do the analysis. This isn't a game to them. They truly care about their research, the spirits and their clients.

When I was asked to give my own personal conclusion to this journey, I had to give it a lot of thought. I kept thinking about what Pop once said to me "They are there, they do exist but it's up to you to decide why". So with that in mind, my opinion is ghost or spirits are definitely out there. I consider them to simply be energy left over from the life they once lived. I believe that their souls have moved on and in spite of that, the spirit of which they once were still remains.

Paranormal research should be ranked up there as one of the true mysteries left on earth. My view is that the supernatural world is unchartered territory. With so many unanswered questions lingering, why would anyone want to stop searching for answers to this incredible mystery? Until there is enough evidence to change the theory that ghost exist into fact, paranormal researchers will be out there researching. It takes dedicated individuals to continue trying to test the boundaries of the unknown and gather enough solid evidence to change a theory into a reality. With as hard as the CTPS group works, I wouldn't put it pass them to be the group to accomplish this. Only time will tell.

      Thanks for the ride, guys!
      Erin O Wallace

Their Equipment

Digital Mini DV Cameras w/Infrared Lights
Digital Hi 8 Cameras w/Infrared Lights
Digital Still Cameras
Thermal Imaging Cameras
Full Spectrum Cameras
Infrared Remote Cameras
Digital Analog Voice Recorders
Wireless Video
Wireless Audio
Electromagnetic Field Meters
Laser Thermometers
Laser Lights
Infrared Night Scopes
Infrared Strobe Lights
Tri-Field Meters
K2 Meters
Motion Detectors
DVR Surveillance System
Two Way Radios
OUIJA/SPRITE BOARDS ARE NEVER USED

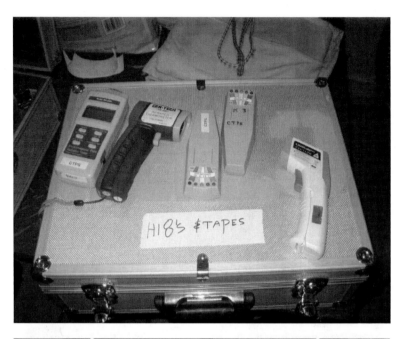

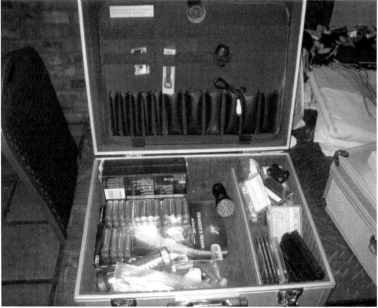

About the Author

Erin O. Wallace - Author / Genealogist / Historical Researcher. She is an award winning writer specializing in newspaper and magazine articles. She is a fifth generation Texan, born and raised in San Antonio. She is a mother of two and grandmother of one. As a child, her own grandmother (Marguerite Zuercher) shared the many stories of her German ancestors as being one of the original families who founded New Braunfels, Texas. She learned of their struggles and hardships as early settlers. It was from those memories that guided her to become a local historian. Her passion for discovering more of her own family's history led her to become a syndicated genealogical columnist.

We are here to help!

CTPS
http://www.ctghost.org